No Easy Answers:
Bayard Rustin
and the
Civil Rights
Movement

No Easy Answers:
Bayard Rustin
and the
Civil Rights
Movement

Calvin Craig Miller

MORGAN
REYNOLDS
Publishing, Inc.

620 South Elm Street, Suite 223
Greensboro, North Carolina 27406
http://www.morganreynolds.com

Portraits of
Black Americans

Bayard Rustin
A. Philip Randolph
Roy Wilkins
W. E. B. Du Bois
Gwendolyn Brooks
Marcus Garvey
William Grant Still
Richard Wright
Thurgood Marshall
Langston Hughes
John Coltrane

NO EASY ANSWERS: BAYARD RUSTIN AND THE CIVIL RIGHTS MOVEMENT

Library of Congress Cataloging-in-Publication Data

Miller, Calvin Craig, 1954-
    No easy answers : Bayard Rustin and the civil rights movement / Calvin Craig Miller.— 1st ed.
      p. cm.
    Includes bibliographical references and index.
    ISBN 1-931798-43-5 (library binding)
    1. Rustin, Bayard, 1912-1987—Juvenile literature. 2. African American civil rights workers—Biography—Juvenile literature. 3. Civil rights workers—United States—Biography—Juvenile literature. 4. African Americans—Civil rights—Juvenile literature. 5. Civil rights movements—United States—History—20th century—Juvenile literature. I. Title.
    E185.97.R93M55 2005
    323'.092—dc22

                                    2004018518

Cover photographs by Warren K. Leffler, courtesy of the Library of Congress.

Contents

One

Morning of Freedom

The streets of Washington, D.C., stood nearly deserted in the early morning of August 28, 1963. Thousands of city residents stayed inside their homes, even though it was a working day. Some had left Washington, going to stay with friends and relatives in Virginia or Delaware. More than a few members of Congress had found pressing business to attend to outside the capital.

One group of Washington professionals stuck to their duties that morning. They were the reporters, photographers and television camera people assigned to cover the March on Washington for Jobs and Freedom. Numerous writers would describe the atmosphere as that of a besieged city, as though the country were at war. Yet the force that caused such anxiety was one that carried no weapons.

Opposite: Bayard Rustin *(Courtesy of Corbis.)*

Its leaders promised a peaceful march, one that broke no laws. Its speakers planned to ask for simple, basic rights for African Americans—a chance to cast their ballots in elections, to live and go to school in the same neighborhoods and schools as whites, to get job training, and to earn a minimum wage.

Such rights are considered so basic today that the fear that August morning seems hard to understand. But black Americans lived in a different world in the early 1960s. Just that past spring, marchers in Birmingham, Alabama, had made similar demands and been attacked by police dogs, shocked with cattle prods, beaten, and jailed. The barbaric spectacle had played out in front of television cameras, sending images of officially sanctioned violence against unarmed demonstrators across the nation and abroad. Washington was not Birmingham, but citizens and legislators in the capital feared that the march would spread violence at the center of government.

A little before 6 AM, Bayard Rustin walked to the base of the Washington Monument. He was a tall, broad-shouldered man with a thin mustache who carried himself with the confidence of an athlete, muscular but graceful. He looked at a crowd of perhaps two hundred milling around the monument, and did not like what he saw.

Bayard had thrown all his energies into organizing this event. He had told reporters that the crowd for the march would top one hundred thousand people. When

The March on Washington. *(Library of Congress)*

they converged on him asking where all the marchers were, he remained outwardly calm. He took out a piece of paper, studied it, and announced, "Gentlemen, everything is going exactly according to plan."

A march volunteer looked at the sheet before Rustin stuffed it back into his pocket. It was blank.

Bayard was bluffing, but the coming hours would prove his faith was justified. Even as he spoke, cars and buses filled with demonstrators poured down the interstate highways into Washington, D.C.

By nine-thirty, forty thousand demonstrators had arrived at the monument, and an hour later, the crowd had more than doubled. Before noon, the march had far outstripped even Bayard's estimates, with more than 250,000 gathered in Washington's streets. At the base of the mall, Hollywood celebrities such as Marlon Brando, Paul Newman, Sydney Poitier, and Charlton Heston were announced as they arrived. Folk singers Joan Baez, Bob Dylan, and others sang to the crowd.

Around midday, a procession to the Lincoln Memorial began. Picket signs proclaimed the goals of the march in uncompromising terms: "Equal Rights, NOW," "Jobs for All, NOW," "Integrated

A. Philip Randolph. *(Library of Congress)*

Schools, NOW," "Voting Rights, NOW," "Freedom Rights, NOW."

A. Philip Randolph, a pioneer of the civil rights movement who had founded the Brotherhood of Sleeping Car Porters, one of the first black unions, delivered the keynote address. "We are not a mob," he declared. "We are the advance guard of a massive moral revolu-

Martin Luther King Jr. giving his famous "I have a dream" speech.

tion for jobs and freedom." The revolution in society would help not just African Americans but everyone, "for our white allies know they cannot be free while we are not."

The list of speakers ran long, as did the speeches. But almost everyone stayed to hear the last person at the podium, Dr. Martin Luther King. King had led the marchers who had been attacked by the police in Birmingham, and he had helped desegregate the buses of Montgomery, Alabama. He was a charismatic and inspiring speaker, trained for a career at the pulpit, and turned by the forces of history into a leader of the civil rights movement.

The speech he gave that day was his historic "I have a dream" address, which described his dream of an America filled with opportunity for all races, one not divided by lines of race. He had a prepared text, but when he departed from it to deliver an extemporaneous

President Kennedy with march organizers. King is to the far left, Randolph to the far right. Rustin, after all the work he did to make the event a success, is conspicuously absent.

line or two in the style of the Bible, he heard encouragement from his audience. His final words were a declaration of deliverance that rings out to this day: "Free at last! Free at last! Thank God Almighty, we are free at last."

As the day wound to a close, King, Randolph, and other march leaders met at the White House with President John F. Kennedy. Bayard was not among them. Instead, he attended to the inglorious details that had fallen to him during his many years as a social activist. There was a simple, brutal reason for Rustin's absence at the White House that historic day. In addition to being black, Rustin carried another stigma in America of 1963: he was an acknowledged homosexual who had to labor in the shadows while others enjoyed the limelight. While the marchers returned home and a select few talked with the president, Bayard supervised the litter crews, making sure that the streets were as clean as the March on Washington had found them.

Two

Early Lessons

Bayard Taylor Rustin was born on March 17, 1912, in the town of West Chester, Pennsylvania. He grew up in the busy, crowded, but loving household of Janifer and Julia Davis Rustin—Ma and Pa to young Bayard.

When he was eleven, however, Bayard (pronounced "Buy-ard") made a surprising discovery about his family. The people he had thought were his parents were actually his grandparents, and his "sister" Florence was actually his mother. He had been born out of wedlock when Florence was a teenager, and his grandparents had decided Bayard would have a better life if they raised him as their own.

Janifer Rustin had been born into slavery, in 1864—one year before the Civil War ended. Janifer had to leave his family behind in Maryland to move to Pennsylvania,

Janifer Rustin, Bayard's grandfather. *(Bayard Rustin Estate)*

but West Chester held many attractions for a young black man. The Quakers there had opposed slavery, and many had offered their homes as sanctuaries for escaping slaves on the Underground Railroad. Some African Americans had even lived there as free citizens well before the Emancipation Proclamation.

Julia Davis's family had lived in West Chester for generations. Julia's mother, Elizabeth, worked as a domestic in the house of the Butlers, a well-to-do white family. Julia's high cheekbones showed the influence of mixed ancestry, a mark of the unions between her family and Delaware Indians. The Butlers helped in Julia's upbringing, sending her to be educated at the local Friends School. She was one of the first in West Chester's black community to graduate from high school. Julia also learned the skills of a practicing nurse.

Quakers made it their mission not only to help free slaves but also to convert them to Quakerism. A man named George Fox founded the sect in England in the middle of the seventeenth century, acting on his belief that religious seekers should be guided by their "inner light" rather than priests. Fox's followers referred to themselves as the Religious Society of Friends. The first to call them Quakers were their enemies, making fun of their habit of trembling during religious services. The Friends simply accepted the jibes and soon enough began to refer to themselves as Quakers.

Quakers held services without the use of rites or ordained ministers. They believed war did harm to the spirit, and many of them refused to serve in the military. They considered all of humanity as one family, so the West Chester Quakers extended their ministry to both Delaware Indians and freed blacks. Their support of African-American rights, however, did not extend to the integration of their religious services. Black Quakers could attend white meetings, but they had to sit in separate sections from whites. Julia Rustin, like many other African Americans, soon left the Friends to join the African Methodist Episcopal (A.M.E.) Church. Even so, Quakerism helped shape her beliefs, among them the Quaker doctrine of pacifism.

Janifer and Julia married in 1891, when she was still a teenager. They would have six daughters and two sons—Anna, Bessie, Earl, Florence, Janifer Junior, Rhetta, Ruth, and Vella. They lived in a succession of houses in respectable neighborhoods. One of their neighbors recalled pleasant childhood memories of the Rustin household.

"They were a fine family in a mixed neighborhood," said Nicholas Tavani, who lived a block from them on North New Street. "We all got along very well. They occupied an old two-story house, with a crab apple tree in front. Old Mr. Rustin allowed us kids to come in and pick crab apples." West Chester embodied the melting-pot tradition of America, becoming home to an assortment of ethnic groups and immigrants. Long before it was customary for races to mix socially, Bayard would grow up thinking that it was nothing unusual to have white friends.

When Florence Rustin was still in her teens, she began dating a laborer named Archie Hopkins. On March 17, 1912, she gave birth to Bayard. The black community in West Chester was close-knit, enough so that Bayard knew Hopkins. He later recalled that his birth father "drank an inordinate amount, gambled an inordinate amount, and played around with girls an inordinate amount." A man with such habits would have made a poor fit in the hard-working and pious Rustin family.

Julia initially chaffed at the idea of having to raise her daughter's child as her own. Anna, one of the Rustin daughters, later said, "At first my mother said 'Oh, I'm just going to let Florence raise that baby by herself.' But one day when she looked down at him in his crib, he smiled up sweetly at her. She decided then and there that Florence could not be a suitable parent, that she would take the baby and raise him properly. All of us pitched in and helped Ma and Pa Rustin to rear Bayard."

Florence Rustin later married and moved to Philadelphia. She and Bayard seldom met or even exchanged letters. He referred to her children as his cousins. If he ever missed his biological mother, he showed few signs of it. Bayard lived a happy and prosperous childhood with his grandparents. The family had earned respect in the community. Janifer showed moderation even in his vices, drinking a little bourbon every night before bed and smoking an occasional cigar. He worked as a caterer for wealthy white families and at the Elks lodge. His business and connections helped raise the family's standard of living. One of the wealthy families that he catered to rented the Rustins a ten-room house on the east side of town, a predominantly African-American neighborhood. The Rustins' home was where prominent black Americans stayed when they came through town, including the famed writer and activist W. E. B. Du Bois.

W. E. B. Du Bois.

Bayard started helping in the family business as soon as he grew old enough to stir mayonnaise and lay out plates and silverware. The catering business provided a bountiful side benefit, allowing the Rustins to dine on food left over from the feasts of the wealthy. Bayard and his siblings grew up eating such delicacies as lobster Newburg, turtle soup, and paté de foie gras.

Julia kept many of her Quaker ways, even finding forgiveness for racists. She became one of the leaders in the local chapter of the National Association for the Advancement of Colored People (NAACP), one of the first groups to fight for African-American equality. She was a slender woman with delicate features, but dominant in personality and determined in her beliefs. "She towered whenever she walked into a room," Bayard recalled. She founded a day nursery, served on the board of a black nurses' group, and set up a summer Bible camp.

Bayard first attended Gay Street Elementary School, then West Chester Junior High School. Like most West Chester public institutions, both were segregated, although some of the instructors were white. The schools boasted excellent teachers, many of whom made race relations part of their lessons. Warren Burton taught mathematics and music. He not only showed Bayard how to read sheet music but also told him about the struggles of blacks in America and their African heritage. Bayard's favorite teacher was Maria Brock, who taught English and elocution. She was the first to introduce him to the writing, debating, and public-speaking skills he would later use to great benefit.

Brock spoke in a refined manner. Her influence may have caused Bayard to adapt a speech habit that his classmates at first considered odd. He began speaking with an upper-class British accent. His friends did not quite know what to make of it.

"Bayard started coming on with what some of us described as funny language," recalled classmate Charles Porter. "He would always be saying 'cahn't' when the rest of us were saying 'cain't.' I think he was picking up his new way of speaking from Miss Brock. Coming from a very educated background, she wanted to raise us above the ordinary cultural standards to which we were accustomed."

Despite his teachers' warnings that discrimination was wrong, young Bayard took part in a seemingly mischievous prank that he later realized was a form of racism. When he was in the fifth grade, he joined with a group of white boys to stand outside a Chinese family's hand laundry, chanting racist taunts and throwing pebbles through the open door of the business.

"I cannot account for how it happened, because I knew it was the wrong thing to do," he said later. Punishment followed swiftly when the father of the family reported Bayard's behavior to the Rustins. Janifer and Julia made Bayard work for free for two weeks in the business of the family he had insulted. Worse than his punishment was Bayard's shame at having failed his grandparents.

In 1930, Bayard enrolled in West Chester Senior High School. The school was integrated, providing its handful of black students a rare chance to cross the color barriers that divided the town. He earned a reputation as a gifted student with a special talent for speaking. Many black students dropped out of school, believing that education beyond primary school did not help young men and women in a segregated society, unless they wanted careers in teaching or nursing. Bayard did not share that view.

"He had ambition and a great feeling about possibility," said former classmate Oliver Patterson. "His determination was extraordinary. He had to prove he was inferior to no one. He had to do what anybody said he couldn't do. If he fell down six flights of stairs, he would get up and tell you how good it felt landing six flights down. And you would almost believe him. That's why he excelled in so many things in high school."

Bayard did well in music, refining his tenor voice in the chorus and glee club. When the chorus competed in a state event at Temple University, he performed as tenor soloist, and West Chester High won all-state honors. He sang so well that many of his peers thought he would pursue a musical career.

He enjoyed athletics too, but found that some sports carried more prestige than others for young men. He was an excellent tennis player, but soon realized that football had more cachet. He went out for that, earning a spot on the offensive line.

"In scrimmages, I found it impossible to get by him," said former teammate John Rodgers. "Sometimes, after knocking me down on my face, he would gently help me to my feet and recite a line or two of poetry." Another player described Bayard as the hardest hitter on the team, an odd role for a teen raised as a pacifist. He helped the West Chester Warriors achieve their first undefeated season in school history. He also ran track, becoming the top sprinter on the team and representing his school at major meets at Franklin Field in Philadelphia.

Sports and music made heavy demands on his time. Floyd Hart, Bayard's music teacher, taught him that the best way to train his voice was to perform the classics. Most black singers were expected to sing spirituals, the traditional religious songs of slaves and their descendents in the South. "Quite frankly, I then regarded spirituals as being rather simplistic," Rustin said later. "Much more study was required when you were doing Bach, Brahms, Schubert, Donizetti, and the others."

Rustin's high school football squad. He is pictured third from the right in the front row. (Chester County Historical Society)

PHILADELPHIA SUBURBAN CHAMPIONS

The respect he earned in chorus, in the classroom, and on athletic fields, however, made little difference when he tried to transcend race barriers in West Chester. White classmates frequently came as guests to the Rustin home, but Bayard did not get invitations to theirs. He could not be served in a white restaurant or buy clothes in a white store. He could attend movies, but only as long as he sat in the balcony reserved for blacks. Such prejudice infuriated him, and he did not always endure it passively. At the Warner theater on South High Street, he was arrested for trying to sit in the white section. It was the first of twenty-five similar arrests in his life.

Bayard attracted a group of friends and followers who shared his sense of injustice at prejudice. They would sit outside Spriggs Restaurant on Market Street and talk about the issues of the day, including race and segregation. On several occasions, he persuaded his friends to join him in taking a stand against unfair treatment.

When the track team traveled to Altoona for a meet, the black athletes were told they would have to stay in a separate hotel. Bayard and his friends balked at the insult. They told coach Harold Zimmerman that they would not compete if the blacks were not admitted to the main hotel. Zimmerman could be an intimidating man who would slam a player against a locker if he did not like his attitude. He might not have cared for the attitude of Bayard's group either, but he did want to compete with a full squad. Zimmerman persuaded the hotel management to accept the black players. On the heels of this small triumph came a petty slight: none of the black players got the pin they were to have received for participating.

In June of 1932, Rustin graduated from West Chester High School, nineteenth out of a little over one hundred students. He also won the D. Webster Meredith Award for public speaking. He was the first black student to do so. Bayard was among six students chosen to speak at the graduation ceremonies. He also sang at the commencement.

Shortly before graduation, Bayard wrote a poem about the way he would like to be remembered after his death. The first stanza reads:

> I ask of you no shining gold;
> I seek not epitaph or fame;
> No monument of stone for me,
> For man need never speak my name.

The poem went on to ask that only an evergreen be planted in remembrance. Bayard's lines foreshadowed his life more than he knew. But after graduation, he faced more immediate concerns than his place in history. He would have enough problems trying to continue his education, a difficult task in a society where expectations remained low for young black men—even those as talented as Rustin.

Three

Young Radical

Bayard Rustin faced two obstacles in seeking a college education in 1932. One of them, of course, was race. The other was the state of the American economy, rocked by the Great Depression.

The Depression began in October 1929, with the dramatic fall of prices on the New York Stock Exchange. Stock prices continued to drop for the next three years, wiping out many investors. By 1933, eleven thousand of the country's twenty-five thousand banks had closed. Today the federal government insures bank customers against the loss of their accounts, but that was not the case in the 1930s. When a bank shut down, people simply lost their money. Spending dropped as the ripple effects of the economic catastrophe spread, causing factories and stores to close. Almost a third of Ameri-

The African-American painter Jacob Lawrence was famous for his depiction of the poverty that ravaged Harlem during the Great Depression. *(Courtesy of Gwendolyn Knight Lawrence / Art Resource.)*

can workers lost their jobs. The nation would not recover for nearly ten years.

Julia Rustin went to work trying to help her grandson, seeking some benefactor willing to help send him to school. She hoped to find him a scholarship based on his excellent high school record, but there were few to be had. A local Rotary Club offered one hundred dollars, but even then, that sum was small compared to the expenses of higher education. She persevered until a meeting with a wealthy church leader in Philadelphia proved fruitful. Dr. R. R. Wright of the A.M.E. Church had just become president of Wilberforce University, an African-American college outside Xenia, Ohio. Wright had heard Rustin sing and arranged for him to get a music scholarship. Rustin eventually left for school, five hundred miles away, with "a pair of chino pants, three shirts and . . . $100."

The Methodist Episcopal Conference of Cincinnati founded Wilberforce, named for William Wilberforce, an English abolitionist, in 1856. It was the first college in the United States established for freed black students. Wilberforce's enrollment was disrupted by the outbreak of the Civil War in 1860. The school temporarily shut down, then was bought by the A.M.E. Church, giving Wilberforce the distinction of being the first American college owned and operated by African Americans.

Rustin added his magnificent tenor voice to the school octet. The Wilberforce singers traveled around the country, helping to raise money for the university. They journeyed to Ohio, Pennsylvania, New York, and the Southern states. They performed spirituals for A.M.E. church groups. Although he had originally disdained spirituals, Rustin came to enjoy them. The songs were very popular with the congregations entertained by the Wilberforce singers and helped them to raise funds.

It was at Wilberforce that Rustin realized he was gay. He formed a close friendship with a male classmate from

The Wilberforce Quartet, a smaller group Rustin sang with in addition to the octet. He is pictured on the far right.

California who sometimes went home with him on vacations. Their relationship was not sexual, but it helped Rustin to come to terms with his sexuality. He talked with his grandmother Julia about his feelings: "I never said 'You know, I'm gay.' I told her I enjoyed being with guys when I joined the parties for dating. And she said 'Is that what you really enjoy?' I said 'Yes, I think I do.' Her reply was 'Then I suppose that's what you need to do.' It wasn't an encouragement, but it was a recognition. So I never felt the need to do a great deal of pretending. And I never had any feelings of guilt."

Rustin's enrollment in Wilberforce lasted barely over a year. For reasons that have never been fully explained, he was asked to leave by the campus administration. He refused to take part in the ROTC drills required at the university, a natural response considering his pacifist upbringing, but one that no doubt cast a poor reflection on him in the eyes of some faculty. He also had organized a strike protesting the poor quality of the food, another conflict that could have hastened his departure. A classmate later suggested that Rustin had developed a crush on the son of the college president, which could have been the reason he was asked to leave. None of these possible explanations, however, have been confirmed.

In 1934, Rustin transferred to Cheyney State Teachers College, not far from his hometown of West Chester. Founded as the Institute for Colored Youth, the Quaker college had originally trained African-American students for manual and agricultural jobs. By the time Rustin enrolled there, Cheyney had shifted its central mission to the training of African-American teachers.

Although enrolled at a teachers college, Bayard was still not sure what career he wanted to follow. All his music teachers had told him that he could have a career as a singer if he applied himself. Then again, both his upbringing and instincts drew him to social activism. For a while, he explored the range of possibilities, earning good grades in the classroom, becoming the star member of the debate team, and singing in the chorus.

But again, he committed some offense that displeased the administration and he was dismissed from Cheyney. As at Wilberforce, the reasons were unclear. What is known is that the college president called him into his office and personally demanded that Rustin withdraw.

He returned to West Chester, as uncertain as ever about the course of his life. Rustin took some odd jobs, including working for a landscaper. But he knew his life's ambition would not be fulfilled by manual labor.

He began making trips to Philadelphia, where he first met members of America's Communist Party.

Communists believe that workers, not corporations or companies, should own the property of a nation. Everyone would contribute to the good of the community to the best of his or her abilities and would, in turn, receive goods and services according to his or her needs. In the 1930s, the Soviet Union was the only major country in the world controlled by Communists, under the leadership of the dictator Joseph Stalin. Communism, as practiced in the Soviet Union, was not consistent with the theories developed by communism's founders, but the true extent of Stalin's abuses was not yet fully known. Many people in the United States were attracted to communism because it promised equality and freedom. Rustin went to some meetings and was intrigued by what he heard, particularly the Communists' opposition to racism. They suggested he go to City College in New York, where tuition was free. He could both further his political education and spread their message.

Well before his dismissal from Cheyney, Rustin knew that he did not want to spend his life in West Chester. In the winter of 1937, he made arrangements to stay with an aunt, Bessie LeBon, and left for Harlem.

Harlem, an area of northern Manhattan, was one of the most vibrant hubs of African-American culture in America. The 1920s were known as the Harlem Renaissance. African Americans from the South and abroad flooded into the area, creating a rich and flourishing

This painting, entitled *Saturday Night Street Scene,* was painted in 1936 by Archibald J. Motley Jr., a forefather of the Harlem Renaissance and one of the first artists to focus on African-American life.

culture of writing, art, and music. Harlem's dance clubs were packed with devotees of swing music. The famous big bands of Duke Ellington and Chick Webb blared loudly enough against the walls of the Savoy to be heard down the street. People arriving from other cities began dancing as soon as they got off the trains.

A group of young people made 151st Street and Convent Avenue their hangout spot. Rustin simply walked up one day and began talking as though he was one of the crowd. At first, they didn't know what to make of him, with his fountain of chatter on controversial issues, delivered in his acquired British accent. They gave him the nickname "English," thinking that he must have come from Great Britain.

Despite the Depression, Rustin managed to live fairly

well. He took temporary jobs such as working for the government's Works Progress Administration (WPA) and serving as a theater usher. He liked socializing while working. An usher whose shift followed Bayard's would often come in to find him enthusiastically conversing with the patrons about stories in the news. From the WPA, he made what might seem a meager salary— $42.50 a week. "That doesn't sound like much, but during the Depression, you could live fairly well on it," Rustin recalled later. "Along 125th Street, you could get a hot dog and a big mug of beer for a nickel. So even when you were down to your last ten cents, you could buy your lunch. Besides, the bars gave out free cheese, free salami, free pickles, and free crackers."

In the spring of 1938, Rustin enrolled in City College of New York (CCNY) in West Harlem. From the outset, he seemed more interested in exploring subjects that interested him than in getting a degree. He decided to audit most of his courses. Rustin declined to take exams in subjects he found boring, but sat for tests in classes that intrigued him, such as economics. By now, Rustin was beginning to realize that he would not be happy as a singer or teacher. Everything in his agenda at City College pointed toward one goal—a career as a social activist.

Rustin soon became involved with the Young Communist League (YCL). He had seen the effects of race inequality in America, and readily saw the comparison with discrimination against the poor and working classes. Though Joseph Stalin would eventually be denounced for using the politics of economic equality to further his harsh and often murderous political agenda, the communists were one of the few groups in America that combined their economic ideals with a firm stand against racism in the late 1930s.

In his early years with the communists, Bayard believed they would fight as hard against racism as they did against rule by the wealthy. The Young Communist League raised that hope when they took on the legal battle of the "Scottsboro Boys," nine young black men and boys accused of raping two women in Alabama.

The case began with a brawl in a boxcar on March 25, 1931, near Scottsboro, Alabama. Two groups of people

The nine "Scottsboro Boys" and their attorney, surrounded by guards. *(Library of Congress)*

riding the rails—one African-American, one white—got into a fight. The white men were outnumbered and thrown off the train. The sheriff was alerted. He stopped the train and arrested nine black men. When they were taken to jail, two young women appeared and one accused some of the men of raping her. The jailers assumed that if they raped one woman, they had probably raped both.

The accused did not even see a defense attorney until their first day in court. Fifteen days after being charged, all but one of the Scottsboro Nine had been sentenced to death. After decades of lynching and lightning-swift convictions of black defendants, this case appeared to be yet another courtroom atrocity in the South. The Young Communist League, along with the American Communist Party, quickly came to the aid of the Scottsboro Boys. The YCL held campus rallies to support them and raise money for their defense.

Medical evidence later refuted the rape charges and one of the women recanted her story and became a speaker at rallies to free the Scottsboro defendants. (They were called the Scottsboro Boys not only because of their youth—the youngest was only twelve years old—but because of the then-common practice of referring to adult African-American men as "boys.") Despite the efforts of the Communist Party and, later, the National Association for the Advancement of Colored People, the Scottsboro Boys all endured years in prison before they finally escaped or were paroled. Their case remains a symbol of injustice, but it also proved there were people willing to challenge the racist and deeply corrupt system. The Communist Party saw a sharp increase in membership as a result.

Bayard Rustin organized chapters (or "cells") of the YCL on his own campus and others, and also helped get its members into the City College Senate and on the staff of the campus newspaper. The YCL office was in a dark alcove in the basement of CCNY, one of many political student groups that honeycombed that level. Organizers for a wide array of causes on both the right and the left used their alcoves to write pamphlets, organize meetings, trade opinions, and argue endlessly. Political discussions could become so heated that they erupted in fistfights. Bayard thrived in the political frenzy.

The YCL gave Bayard an assignment he particularly enjoyed: the formation of the Committee Against Discrimination in the Armed Forces. At the time, African-American soldiers slept in segregated barracks, fought in all-black units, and were often assigned the most dangerous missions. Raised in the Quaker tradition, Bayard did not advocate war for any reason. But he did think that black and white soldiers should be treated equally.

Bayard's mission was of key importance as nations edged toward World War II. Adolf Hitler had come to power in Germany, Benito Mussolini in Italy. Both hurled threats of military aggression at bordering nations. President Franklin Roosevelt had once promised to keep the U.S. out of any European war, but his promises seemed less secure as Hitler and Mussolini grew bolder. The YCL was convinced that Roosevelt wanted a war so he could protect the interests of American capitalists.

While organizing for the controversial YCL, Rustin continued to socialize with his friends from the street corners, some of whom could not have cared less about politics. "I used to follow Bayard when he visited a communist cell at 146th Street near Saint Nicholas Avenue," his friend Howard Wallace recalled. "The cell was right next door to a place called Kirby's Pool Room. When you were broke and had nothing, that was a good place to go. The people there were friendly. Whatever they had to eat and drink, they shared with you. Bayard was like a big sport. Whenever we went into Williamson's Restaurant, on 150th Street, he would treat everybody."

Rustin enjoyed being a regular guy, but also believed that his talents would take him well beyond the ambitions of his street buddies. His experiences in New York only increased his self-confidence. Sometimes good fortune almost seemed to fall into his lap.

Leonard DePaur, who was auditioning singers for an all-black Broadway musical, heard Rustin singing spirituals at Mother A.M.E. Zion Church in Harlem. He later asked Rustin to join the cast of *John Henry,* starring internationally acclaimed singer and actor Paul Robeson. Rustin was delighted. He would earn not only a regular paycheck but also the distinction of performing with a musical legend. Critics did not give good reviews to the play, however, and it closed after a short run.

Nonetheless, Rustin proved that the classmates and teachers who predicted he could have a career in music might have been right. He went on to join the Carolinians, a group formed by Josh White, the guitarist and singer who had played the main supporting role in *John Henry*. Columbia Records signed the group and released their album *Chain Gang*. The album did not sell well. Rustin continued to sing in clubs for a while with the Carolinians, but he focused his main efforts on organizing for the YCL.

One of Bayard's albums.

While working for the communists, Bayard met a social reformer he admired as much as any celebrity. A. Philip Randolph, born in 1889, was the most successful black union organizer in the United States. White workers had enjoyed the protection of labor unions for years, but unions did not always admit African Americans. When several white unions formed the American Federation of Labor (AFL) in 1886, the labor movement gained the strength it needed to improve pay and working conditions. Labor leaders could speak for their whole membership, setting up a process of collective

Randolph's group, the Brotherhood of Sleeping Car Porters, was one of the first African-American unions. *(Library of Congress)*

bargaining to settle disputes with management. If a company resisted bargaining with workers, the union could call a strike: employees would refuse to do their jobs until the dispute was settled.

In 1925, Randolph founded the Brotherhood of Sleeping Car Porters (BSCP), the first black trade union. He succeeded in merging his union with the AFL at a time when half the labor unions in the country would not accept black members. The BSCP negotiated its first contract with the Pullman Company in 1937.

Randolph had grown up in Jacksonville, Florida, a city where races mixed more freely than elsewhere in the South. His father was a minister who taught his children never to use segregated facilities in public places and to resist racial discrimination in their daily lives. To supplement his meager income from preaching, the Reverend James William Randolph sold firewood and fresh meat, but his sense of charity was so great that it hurt him as a businessman. He extended credit to poor families and might have plunged the Randolphs into destitution had his wife Elizabeth not stopped the policy. A. Philip Randolph inherited his father's belief that money was not the most important thing in life. Reverend Randolph also taught his two sons to speak clearly and carry themselves with good posture.

Like Randolph, Rustin believed that economic discrimination was one of the most damaging effects of racism. After reading about Randolph, Rustin went to his office on West 125ᵗʰ Street to try to meet the man. He stood in awe of Randolph's reputation and accomplishments, and felt himself a nobody by comparison. Rustin had heard reports that Randolph was stiff and aloof in person, but Randolph surprised his young guest with his gentlemanly and friendly reception. "This man of great dignity and inner beauty," Rustin later recalled, "stood up, walked from behind his desk, met me in the middle of the room, shook hands and offered me a seat." Randolph swiped his hand several times in the air over the chair, in a courtly gesture that created the impression that he was dusting the seat for his visitor.

Randolph's background was much like his young visitor's. Of course, they also shared a commitment to racial equality. Furthermore, Randolph had roots in the A.M.E. Church in Florida, just as Rustin had in West Chester. Both had attended City College and been drawn to radical causes.

Their differences were just as important, however. Randolph's youthful activism was based on the tenets of socialism, while Rustin was fueled by the ideas of the Communist Party. While socialism and communism have the same ultimate goals, socialists were considered more temperate, while communists advocated revolutionary change.

In capitalist countries, such as the United States, the government allows the economy to be regulated by the free market. Anyone who can produce a product or service can sell it for the maximum price consumers are willing to pay. Businesses charge more for a product than it costs them to produce it in order to make profits. Prices are kept in check by competition.

Both socialists and communists criticized the free market system, charging that it was "free" only for those wealthy enough to build factories and hire laborers. They believed that property and income should be under social control instead of being controlled by market forces. Communists believed in very similar goals, but they also believed the only way these goals could be achieved was through revolution. In practice, communist governments called for workers to relinquish much of their individual liberty, including criticism of the system, and were often corrupt and poorly managed.

Unlike the young communists, Randolph strongly believed in American democracy. "By fighting for their rights now, American Negroes are helping to make America a moral and spiritual arsenal of democracy," he wrote. African Americans' "fight for economic, political and social equality, thus becomes part of the global war for freedom." An America that extended liberty to all, without regard to race, could more effectively champion democracy throughout the world.

Randolph quickly realized that Rustin was a communist, but wisely held his criticism until the end of their friendly conversation. "I am sorry to know that you are associated with communists because I think you're going to discover they are not interested in civil rights," Randolph said. "They are interested in using civil rights for their own purposes."

Randolph was voicing a common concern about communists, and it was true that they did see the racial struggle mostly in economic terms—as an injustice that could only be corrected by the overthrow of capitalism. Yet communists showed their commitment to racial equality through social activism, such as their protests on behalf of the Scottsboro Nine. Still, Randolph was correct in predicting Rustin's disillusionment with the Young Communist League, a break that was hastened by the war in Europe.

In 1939, Stalin disregarded an existing nonaggression pact and invaded Finland. Rustin thought the Russian invasion wrong. Rustin's common ground with the Young Communist League became even shakier when the YCL's commitment to the Scottsboro Nine began to fade as the war heated up. "That's when I began to smell [that] there was something radically wrong," Rustin later said.

Hitler invaded Russia in June of 1941, in violation of a similar nonaggression pact with the Russians. American Communist groups, including the YCL, began to urge American intervention in the conflict. America would indeed enter the war in December of 1941, after the Japanese bombing of Pearl Harbor. But Rustin refused to organize on behalf of any kind of armed conflict.

The last string holding him to the communists snapped when YCL leaders called him in and told him to draw up a plan for dismantling the Committee Against Discrimination in the Armed Forces. As Rustin saw it, the communists planned to abide racial discrimination in order not to rock the military boat during wartime. He wrote later, "the Communists had now demonstrated that they were not concerned about what was happening in the United States, but what in their view was best for the Soviet Union. They were prepared to sacrifice everything, including the urgent need for improved conditions for Negroes, for the USSR."

Rustin turned in his resignation. At age twenty-nine, he was a radical in search of a movement, but only for a while. His energy and commitment had not escaped the eyes of other social reformers, nor would his talents go to waste.

Four

Ambassador for Peace

Bayard Rustin wasted no time after quitting the Young Communist League. Almost thirty years old, he wanted to get his career as a civil rights activist back on track quickly. In June of 1941, he walked back into the office of the man who had taken him to task for his communist beliefs.

A. Philip Randolph was delighted to take on a fresh recruit, for he had a project with a pressing deadline. He was planning a march on Washington to protest the official policy of all-white defense plants. With the war looming, armaments plants were churning out weapons at full speed, which meant there were plenty of good jobs available—but only for white workers. As he had with the YCL, Bayard found himself in the uncomfortable position of being a pacifist defending African Americans' rights to be a part of the war effort.

The march itself was the kind of bold step that had earned Randolph his renown. He had challenged the top official in the United States, telling President Franklin Delano Roosevelt that he would put civil rights marchers in the streets of Washington if Roosevelt did not sign an executive order prohibiting discrimination in defense-plant hiring. Randolph had set a date of July 1 for the president to either sign the order or trigger the mass march.

Roosevelt did not like being handed ultimatums. He did know of Randolph's prestige in the black community, though, and did not doubt his word. First Lady Eleanor Roosevelt may also have influenced her husband's decision when she returned from a trip to New York where she had seen militant preparations for the march. In the end, the president relented and signed the order, which declared, "there shall be no discrimination in the employment of workers in defense industries or government because of race, creed, color, or national origin."

Randolph then kept his part of the bargain and called off the

Eleanor Roosevelt visited the Tuskegee Army Air Field in 1941, where Charles Alfred Anderson, the first African American to receive his pilot's license, took the First Lady for a flight.

march. To a man of his generation—Randolph was then fifty-two—calling off the march seemed the honorable thing to do. But to some of his young followers, hungry for the chance to show their commitment in the streets, it seemed that Randolph had backed down. They complained about Randolph's decision and attempted to force him to reschedule the march. Rustin was among the dissenters. There had never been a massive demonstration against racial discrimination in the nation's capital, and he thought Randolph was wasting a historic opportunity.

Randolph quelled the rebellion in his own ranks and dressed down those who questioned him. He put out a position paper which clearly explained what he thought of the dissension—it had subtitles including "The Youth Were Too Enamored of the Romantic Flavor of Demonstration" and "Some Members of the Youth Division Were Communist Dupes." Randolph's words must have stung Rustin, for he had once been told, in so many words, that he was also a "dupe" of the communists.

Though taken aback by the rebuke, Rustin nonetheless seized upon the spirit of the march as one of the most enduring landmarks of his activist career. He later called it "the symbolic inauguration of the modern civil rights movement," because it foreshadowed not only the fight against segregation and discrimination that came to a crossroads in the 1950s, but also the civil rights marches of the 1960s.

Rustin left Randolph's movement in the late summer

of 1941. Carrying a long list of social activist credentials in a still-young career, he took a job with a pacifist organization, the Fellowship of Reconciliation. His boss and mentor there was A. J. Muste, a white radical minister.

The Fellowship of Reconciliation (FOR) was a church-based antiwar group that had been born as World War I threatened the continent in the summer of 1914. Protestants in Garden City, Long Island, founded an American branch in November of 1915. The Fellowship did not believe achieving peace was a passive process, gained only by avoiding war. Its members spoke of an active process, "waging peace," through struggle against the forces of militarism.

A. J. Muste was a scholarly, bespectacled man with thinning gray hair at the time Rustin met him. His followers considered him a saint, though many others thought him a raving lunatic. He accepted no compromises in his quest for peace on Christian terms. In the early days of World War II, many ministers used their pulpits to call for victory over Hitler. Muste shocked nearly everyone when he declared, "If I can't love Hitler, I can't love at all." Muste was referring to the Christian doctrine which advocated loving the sinner while hating his sin. Even so, some of the audience was shocked. A Jewish journalist at the meeting pondered the dilemma of such die-hard Christians. "It was hard enough to be a Jew," he later wrote, "even in America, and desperately hard in Germany; but anything was better than having to be a Christian and love your enemies."

Rustin with his mentor, American pacifist A. J. Muste. *(Bayard Rustin Estate)*

Even before being formally employed by FOR, Rustin carried out a mission for Muste in Puerto Rico. He had made arrangements to travel with the American Friends Service Committee, a Quaker organization devoted to peace through public service and information. He was the only black member of an eleven-person group of peace volunteers. Muste wanted to know what problems Puerto Rican conscientious objectors to the war faced. Rustin arrived home in August of 1941 with a thorough report. Muste was greatly impressed.

At the twenty-sixth annual FOR conference a month later, Muste announced three new high-level employees. He named Rustin as secretary for student and general affairs. James Farmer would be the race relations secretary, George Houser the youth secretary. The Reverend Glenn Smiley joined Muste's administrative staff not long afterward. Farmer and Rustin were black, Houser and Smiley white. All of them would make significant contributions in the struggle for racial and social equality.

FOR members often looked to the work of a leader in India in their campaign to wage peace. At the time, Mahatma Gandhi was working to achieve India's independence from British rule. His movement was not a military effort but one based on nonviolent civil disobedience. The philosophy called upon Gandhi's followers to break laws that his movement considered unjust, those that the British had put in place to subjugate Indians. When attacked, confronted, or arrested, however, they would not fight back. They would attempt to communicate with arresting police, even while being assaulted. Gandhi's unorthodox method of rebellion would be vindicated in 1947 when India gained its independence from the British.

No one in the Fellowship of Reconciliation was a more devout disciple of Gandhi than its leader. Muste wrote, "Pacifism with Gandhi [was] not a tool you pick up or lay down, use today but not tomorrow. . . . It was a way of life." Muste was convinced that nonviolent resistance was the only way for pacifism to succeed in America.

Rustin believed that Gandhi's methods could also provide a model for achieving racial equality. He advocated their use in every battle of the struggle for African-American rights. "Next to A. Philip Randolph, Gandhi had more direct influence on the development of a civil rights strategy during the 1940s than any other individual," he later wrote.

Mohandas Karamchand Gandhi ("Mahatma," meaning "great soul," was a title later bestowed on him by his admirers) was born on October 2, 1869, in Porbandar, India. At nineteen, he became a law stu-

Mohandas Karamchand "Mahatma" Gandhi.

dent at University College in London. Because he was Indian, other students shunned him. He spent most of his time alone reading. There he first read the works of such American philosophers as Henry David Thoreau, who advocated "civil disobedience," or the breaking of unjust laws as a matter of conscience. Thoreau's views helped shape Gandhi's methods of resisting oppression without violence.

After graduating, Gandhi practiced law in South Africa. His professional peers considered him a "colored" lawyer because of his brown skin, but he nonetheless built a successful practice. The plight of his fellow Indians abroad disturbed Gandhi. Most often employed as laborers, they were regarded as inferior in both England and Africa.

Ghandi returned to India in 1914. Britain ruled his native country, administrating it as a colony. Gandhi wanted to create a resistance movement that included all levels of the highly stratified Indian society, so he abandoned his Western suits in favor of a loincloth and sandals to demonstrate his solidarity with the lower classes. Gandhi began a campaign of resistance to British rule unlike any the occupiers had ever witnessed. The British had a monopoly on the manufacture of salt, forbidding anyone else to make it. On March 12, 1940, he announced he would march to the sea and make salt. Thousands of his followers joined him.

Gandhi taught his followers not to avoid arrest. Mass arrests soon filled the jails to overflowing, creating a burden on the system. Being arrested became a badge of honor for those seeking to overthrow the British. Gandhi also told Indians not to defend themselves when they were beaten, but to talk to their attackers, forcing those who might hate them to see them as human beings. His methods succeeded in creating a great deal of international sympathy for his movement and embarrassing the British. American racial activists avidly read Gandhi's works and began devising ways his strategy might work to their movement's advantage.

James Farmer, the race relations director of FOR, was another convert to Gandhi's methods. Farmer had traveled far from his roots as a self-described "preacher's kid" from Holly Springs, Mississippi. His father was better educated than most preachers, however, having earned his Ph.D. in a time when even undergraduate college degrees were rare among black people. He taught theology at Rust College, an all-black school in Holly Springs. Farmer's father was well-respected in the African-American community but poorly paid, so the family lived frugally.

Farmer had bristled at the indignities he suffered growing up in Mississippi, hearing racial slurs and insults hurled at him and his family. Like many others, he questioned why blacks had to ride at the backs of buses. Once Farmer had watched in shame as two white men interrupted a family picnic and forced his father to sign over his entire salary check as recompense for accidentally running over a pig. "My heart swelled with rebellion," he wrote later, and he vowed not to put up with such treatment when he came of age.

As race relations secretary of FOR, James Farmer urged its leadership to sponsor a civil rights organization that would use Gandhi's methods to resist racial discrimination. Muste and his lieutenants balked at connecting FOR to an organization beyond its pacifist mission. They approved of the idea in principle, though, and allowed Farmer to continue to work for FOR while founding the new group. In 1942, Farmer founded the Congress of Racial Equality (CORE) at the University of Chicago.

Rustin was enthusiastic about CORE's mission, and

used his organizational skills to give the fledgling organization a hand. CORE carried out the first sit-in in American history, when it integrated the Jack Spratt restaurant in Chicago. Twenty-eight CORE members took seats in the restaurant and refused to leave until they were served. The management called the police, but CORE

CORE founder James Farmer. *(Courtesy of the Library of Congress.)*

had prepared for the confrontation by notifying the police in advance. The officers informed the proprietors that waiting for service was not a crime. Nor was serving black people, at least not in Chicago, and the restaurant reluctantly agreed to serve the protesters. The whole campaign to integrate Jack Spratt had lasted only a few hours.

Most of Rustin's time was spent traveling and speaking on behalf of FOR. He traveled more than 17,000 miles in 1942, crisscrossing twenty states, giving speeches at universities, high schools, and summer camps. A. J.

Muste wanted Rustin to attract converts to pacifism, a difficult task in the midst of World War II. After the Japanese bombed Pearl Harbor, support for military intervention ran high. Still, Rustin lectured to audiences of all races at churches, high schools, college campuses, and civic clubs. While pacifism was the core message, at least in theory, Muste gave Rustin free rein to denounce racism as well. Rustin was eager to take on the task, promoting nonviolence as a tactic against discrimination, the problem of racial exploitation, and the evils of a segregated military.

He gave speeches with titles like "A Minority in Our Democracy," "Race, Religion and Nationalism," and "Can Nonviolent Non-Cooperation Win Freedom for the American Negro?" Rustin infuriated some audience members in Dayton, Ohio, when he said that Hitler was more honest with Jews than President Roosevelt was with blacks, because Hitler never claimed to be a friend of the Jews.

Rustin not only honed his speaking skills but also was able to practice what he preached: he found battling racism was an everyday task for a traveling African American in the 1940s. He encountered discrimination as he tried to rent hotel rooms, ride buses, or even get haircuts. These problems were caused by a system that called for separation of blacks and whites in public places, transportation, and education. The Supreme Court had ruled that states had the right to enforce "separate but equal" laws to keep the races apart. The legal foundation for separate but equal facilities came from so-called Jim Crow laws.

Minstrel shows, performances by white actors wearing black makeup, put the term Jim Crow into common usage in the early 1800s. Thomas Dartmouth Rice performed a routine called "Jump Jim Crow" that

A nineteenth-century drawing of "Jim Crow."

mimicked African-American stereotypes of the time. Jim Crow started out only as an insulting caricature, but became a term for legislation that kept blacks and whites from mixing as equals. Jim Crow laws, passed from the late 1870s through the 1950s, made it illegal for blacks and whites to eat at restaurants, ride buses, or attend school together. They could not even be buried in the same cemeteries. The Supreme Court endorsed these laws because, they said, even though the facilities might be separate, as long as they were "equal" there was no reason to complain.

But in practice, black schools and public facilities were not equal but inferior. Black schools would get

Segregation functioned under the flawed concept of "separate but equal."

secondhand textbooks from white schools, and black businesses would be restricted to the worst sections of town. Jim Crow regulations required that blacks sit in the backs of buses while whites rode up front. Attempts to resist or reform the system were often met with violence, imprisonment, or worse.

Rustin was one of the people who tried to stand up against the Jim Crow laws. He paid the price for his resistance, but he also managed to gain some victories against the system.

At an Indianapolis diner, the waitress refused to serve him or even acknowledge his presence. He complained to the manager, who replied that the restaurant would lose business if she served a black man. He urged the proprietor to test her beliefs: if she would serve him a hamburger, he would sit by the door without touching it for ten or fifteen minutes. If his presence stopped customers from coming in, he would leave.

She agreed. Several customers came in while Rustin ignored his burger, and none appeared to take notice of him. The manager took his cold burger, brought him a fresh one, and the restaurant thereafter dropped its policy of not serving blacks.

Rustin did not always succeed in his attempts to negotiate his way around discrimination, especially in the South, where Jim Crow laws were vigorously enforced. Traveling near Nashville in 1942, he boarded a bus wearing a jacket and red tie, loosened at the neck because of the heat. A woman with a small child sat near the front. As he juggled his baggage, his tie flew out and the child grabbed it.

He later recalled that the mother instantly struck the child and said, "Don't touch a nigger." He was momentarily disarmed by shock, and for once, took a seat in the black section at the back. While pondering what had just happened, he noticed a black couple, sharing a box lunch, chatting cheerfully as though they had not even seen the ugly incident. At that moment, he had an epiphany: "And I said, how many years are we going to sit in the back and let that child be misled by its mother— that if we sit in the back and really are having fun, then whites in a way have the right to say they [African Americans] like it in the back . . . I vowed then and there I was never going through the South again without either being arrested or thrown off the bus or protesting."

He moved to the front. When the bus driver asked him to move, he refused, explaining that he could not cooperate with an unjust law. The driver demanded he move at every stop, but every time Rustin refused. Finally the driver called the police. Just outside of Nashville, four officers boarded the bus. They beat him in front of the other passengers, some of whom begged the police to stop. They took him to the station in Nashville, where the physical abuse continued. Policemen tossed him back and forth along a gauntlet, tearing his clothes, even as Rustin tried to talk with them, following Gandhi's doctrine of trying to communicate with one's attackers.

Rustin's bravery in the face of bigotry accomplished the kind of incremental victory that he had made a goal during his travels. He had shocked at least some of the white passengers into protesting the police beating. One of them even came to the police station to lodge a complaint. The assistant district attorney talked with Rustin and released him without pressing charges.

Not all of the bigotry Bayard experienced came from people who considered themselves bigots. He arrived early for a meeting at a church in Ohio, and quietly took a seat in the back. As the time for the meeting grew closer, church leaders began to search for the speaker. They did not know that Bayard Rustin was a black man.

"When the meeting began, the guest speaker seemed not to be there," recalled John Mecartney, then a young Methodist minister. "Finally, someone said, 'Why don't we ask the Negro janitor sitting back there if he has seen the speaker in any part of the building?' We approached the man and asked him that question. 'I am Bayard Rustin,' he said." Bayard's speech that evening received an enthusiastic reception, and may have convinced his chagrined guests not to make easy assumptions about race roles.

When Rustin spoke in Washington, he had to seek lodging at the homes of other pacifists, for hotels would not accept blacks. Danny Wilcher, a young pacifist who had heard him speak in the Midwest, asked his parents for permission to have him stay at their house. Although his father, a Methodist minister, readily agreed, Wilcher remembers that his "mother, an old sort from Virginia, said 'Son, you can bring him here to stay, but I shall have to leave and spend the night at your sister's apartment. I couldn't spend the night in the same house with a black person.'" Wilcher was very embarrassed by his mother's attitude, but Bayard put him at ease. He understood the reality of race relations in the 1940s and was unruffled by the slight. He also believed it was better to ignore insults than to be angry at them: anger was a wasteful emotion.

Muste was greatly pleased by Rustin's efforts and made plans to set him up for an extended stay in San Francisco—through October and November of 1943. Muste wanted Rustin to get the experience of organizing in one area for a sustained period of time. But the United States' plans for Bayard Rustin clashed with those of the Fellowship of Reconciliation. In mid-November, a draft board of the Selective Service System sent Rustin a notice ordering him to report for his physical examination. They wanted him to go to war.

Five

Prisoner of Conscience

Bayard Rustin refused to be drafted. In doing so, he deliberately took a more difficult path than necessary. He had many options that would have allowed him to stay out of the military without risking imprisonment. He instead chose to speak out in protest and paid heavily, behind bars, for his principled stand.

The military allowed some young men to register as conscientious objectors. Conscientious objectors (COs) could be excused from military duty on religious grounds and assigned to do civilian work instead. The requirements were difficult, but Quakers routinely got such exceptions due to their long tradition of opposing wars. In fact, that was Bayard's original intention. In 1940, he had applied for and been granted conscientious objector status. The draft board notice he received in 1943 simply required that Rustin take a physical examination so that he could be assigned to a Civilian Public Service (CPS) camp. The CPS camps assigned conscientious objectors to perform manual labor, mostly in rural areas.

Three more years of working to resist war had changed Bayard's mind about the justice of taking a conscientious objector's exemption. He now believed that a person should be allowed to refuse to serve in the military simply on moral grounds, without belonging to any religious group. It also troubled him that the military supervised the CPS camps—even though he would not be fighting, he would still be serving a cause he did not believe in.

The draft board also did not offer the right to conscientious objector status equally among all religions. Exemptions were generally granted to Mennonites, Brethren, and Quakers, because of their long history of pacifism. Jehovah's Witnesses who refused to be drafted on religious grounds were imprisoned: their religion had been founded only in 1872 and thus did not qualify as having a long history.

Rustin wrote a defiant letter to the draft board. "I cannot voluntarily submit to an order stemming from the selective service act. War is wrong. . . . Though joyfully following the will of God, I regret that I must break the law of the State. I am prepared for whatever may follow."

What followed was swift punishment. Two months later, on January 12, 1944, a federal marshal arrested Rustin in New York. He went to trial on February 17, and was sentenced to three years in a federal prison. George Houser, Rustin's young colleague at FOR, had drawn a sentence of a year and a day. Rustin may have been given a longer sentence because of his highly visible antiwar stance.

Rustin went first to a detention center on the West Side of Manhattan, then to a penitentiary in Ashland, Kentucky. His colleagues at FOR worried about how Rustin would hold up under the stress of prison. One of them wrote to Rustin's grandmother, Julia, to express sympathy and concern. Julia was worried too, but she replied that she and Bayard had planned to read one of the Psalms simultaneously on his birthday, as a prayer to give him strength. A week after his arrival at the federal penitentiary, Bayard turned thirty-two. At one o'clock in the afternoon, he read Psalm 56, which de-scribes a person fighting against injustice and oppression, and contains the line "In God I trust without a fear: What can man do to me?"

To keep his mind active while in prison, Rustin read magazines and books sent from the outside and taught himself to play the lute. Some of the men liked hearing him play, and he would oblige them with sentimental ballads, even though he liked them less than classical music. His music helped him keep his sanity as he sought to continue his work even while in prison. "When you're dealing with people all the time and nothing is ever settled, it's a pleasure to strike a C chord and know that it's a C chord," he said later. A number of inmates had

entered prison for the same reason as Bayard. He made alliances with other conscientious objectors and black prisoners, protesting their shared injustices.

Some of Bayard's protests were only small gestures. He sang the Billie Holliday song "Strange Fruit" into the pipes of the ventilation system, thus serenading his guards with a ballad about black lynchings. Such actions did not endear him to either his guards or some of the white inmates, who held many of the prejudices that characterized the world outside the prison walls.

Bayard, always a talented musician, took up the lute while in prison. *(Bayard Rustin Estate)*

Prison warden Robert Hagerman was a medical doctor who believed rehabilitation was an important part of a prison's function. Regarded by his colleagues as a liberal, he had become a prison warden to offer service to society. Hagerman agreed to let Rustin teach a class in history to fellow inmates.

Rustin's fifteen students came from the poor rural regions of the South, mostly the Appalachian mountains of Tennessee and Kentucky. Rustin enjoyed teaching. He considered it an opportunity to continue his work to bring the races together. "Being taught by a Negro is for them a revolutionary experience," he said of his students, and added optimistically, "white southerners may be ready for some real progressive changes."

Excited by his success, Rustin pushed Hagerman to desegregate the prison. Black and white prisoners were confined to segregated cellblocks and ate in separate seating areas of the dining hall. Hagerman granted a small concession by instructing guards to leave the gate separating whites from blacks unlocked. Thus any black inmate could mingle with his white counterparts in the common area. None did except for Rustin, who joined the white men on Sundays to listen to radio broadcasts of classical music.

News of Rustin's agitation was infuriating to one of the more violent racists at the Ashland penitentiary. "Judge" Huddleston had achieved success as a state politician in Kentucky before being convicted of fraud. Like other Jim Crow politicians, Huddleston fervently believed in segregation of the races. He seethed with resentment every time Rustin crossed into the white section of the prison. One Sunday, when Rustin came to listen to the radio, Huddleston grabbed a stick about the size of a broom handle and brought it crashing down on Rustin's head.

Rather than defending himself, Rustin chose to resist the attack in the way that Gandhi had taught, covering his head with his hands and refusing to strike back. "You can't hurt me," Bayard told his attacker over and over again. Huddleston's blows became more erratic, hitting other prisoners as the stick shattered. His resolve shattered almost as quickly as his weapon did. He suddenly stopped the beating and sat down, shaken and trembling. Bayard suffered a broken wrist, but his example had taught the other inmates more about nonviolence than a dozen lectures on Gandhi could.

When he entered prison, Rustin was forced to sign a form consenting to have his correspondence and reading materials censored. As a result, not all of his letters made it to their recipients, but instead landed on desks in the Bureau of Prisons in Washington. Rustin came to see censorship as dehumanizing as the threat of violence.

The breaking point came when a censor confiscated his copy of *Equality,* the newsletter of the Congress of Racial Equality. Bayard was enraged. He warned the prison authorities that he had friends on the outside who would "send him stuff by the pound," complicating the censor's job and once again making life difficult for prison authorities. The censor yielded, and Bayard got his next copy of *Equality* without interference.

Rustin's application of civil disobedience and protest was beginning to wear on Warden Hagerman and the prison staff. Guards reported that he had made homosexual advances to other prisoners, charges Hagerman had investigated. The chief medical officer held sessions with Bayard, during which he pressed for details about his sexuality. Bayard admitted his homosexuality, and, after lengthy confrontation, to having affairs with two prisoners.

Other pacifists in prison had kept A. J. Muste abreast of news from the penitentiary. When they wrote to him about the charges Rustin was facing, his old mentor at the Fellowship of Reconciliation showed he was capable of discrimination: "You have been guilty of gross misconduct, specially reprehensible in a person making the claims to leadership and—in a sense—moral superiority which you were making." Muste went on, "you had deceived everybody, including your own comrades and most devoted friends. . . . You were capable of making the 'mistake' of thinking that you could be the leader of a revolution of the most basic and intricate kind at the same time you were a weakling in an extreme degree and engaged in practices for which there was no justification, which a person with a tenth of your brains must have known would defeat your objective."

Like most people of the era, Muste considered homosexuality a choice and saw it as morally reprehensible behavior. Rustin, so quick to protest discrimination based on race, meekly promised Muste he would refrain from any further sexual contact while in prison. The time had not yet come to stand up for gay rights.

Rustin channeled his energy into attempts to desegregate the prison by pushing for integrated tables in the dining hall. After repeatedly defying prison regulations, he was put in solitary confinement. Shortly after his release, the authorities at Ashland transferred Bayard and other pacifists to the penitentiary at Lewisburg, Pennsylvania.

Lewisburg held some of the most hardened criminals in America. Oddly, for a prison that incarcerated people drawn to violent crime, it also had a history of confining pacifists. Warden William Hiatt dealt with numerous conscientious objectors. Hiatt's method was simple: he simply quarantined the COs as if they carried a contagious disease. He had them confined to the library, so that the other inmates would not be infected by their ideas.

Hiatt's velvet-glove approach allowed COs liberties and safety far beyond that offered at Ashland. Guards delivered meals to the library. The prisoners could eat with whomever they chose and read anything they wanted. Bayard needed not fear physical attack, such as the beating Judge Huddleston had inflicted upon him.

Rustin also lost any chance to continue his prison organizing, the main activity that made his experience behind bars meaningful. He knew very well why the warden isolated him away from the general population, and conceded that the status of the conscientious objector was quite different from the ordinary inmate.

"We used to say that the difference between us and other prisoners was the difference between fasting and starving," he recalled. "*We* were there by virtue of a commitment we had made to a moral position; and that gave us a psychological attitude the average prisoner did not have. He felt either that he had done something wrong, and that he should be punished for it, or that he had done nothing wrong, and society was brutalizing him. We had the feeling of being morally important; and that made us respond to prison conditions without fear, with considerable sensitivity to human rights."

Still, prison was prison. Holding the moral high ground did not subtract every measure of punishment. Rustin described aspects of imprisonment common to Ashland, Lewisburg, and every penitentiary in America: "Still, what is oppressive about prison is that one is unable to be a human being. He is unable to make a single decision about anything he thinks is important. A bell rings, and you are permitted to take a shower. A bell rings, and you can go and eat. A bell rings and you can go to the library. A bell rings, and you must leave the library. A bell rings, and you have no lights at night. A bell rings, and you must get up in the morning. A bell rings, and you must leave your cell. A bell rings, and you can go for physical exercise. A bell rings, and you can see the warden. A bell rings, and if you are in the middle of a sentence you must stop talking to the warden. These books you may read and these books you may not read. All of that robs people of their inner capacity to be human beings. And almost all of the violence in prison springs from that."

Two mug shots of Rustin show the stress that life behind bars inflicted upon him. One taken upon his entry into Ashland shows him as a serene young man, clear-eyed and smooth-skinned, with a calm gaze that suggests a sense of mission. Another taken in August of 1945 shows a man wearing a tight frown and a hostile glare.

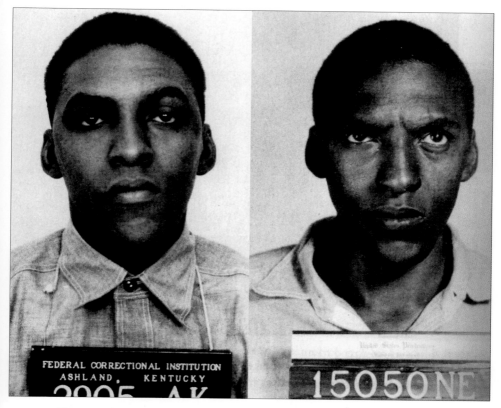

Two mug shots of Rustin. The one on the left was taken in 1944 when he entered prison, the other in August 1945. *(National Archives)*

His face is sharp and angular from weight loss, and there is a hard crease between his eyes and bags beneath them.

Rustin was set free from Lewisburg on June 11, 1946, almost a year after World War II ended. He walked out of the penitentiary gate at 11:20 in the morning, wearing a blue suit. He had twenty dollars in his pocket. He rode the train to Penn Station in Manhattan, where his grandmother Julia joyously embraced him. Now that prison was behind him, he faced a dilemma similar to all inmates who regained their freedom—how to find his place in a world that had changed while he served his time.

Six

Journey of Reconciliation

Only twenty-eight months elapsed between the time Bayard Rustin entered prison and the June day he was released in 1946. But the world he reentered was not the one he had left. Europe's conquering fascist dictators, Adolf Hitler of Germany and Benito Mussolini of Italy, were dead. To end the war with Japan, President Harry Truman had chosen to drop atomic bombs on the cities of Hiroshima and Nagasaki.

The atomic fireballs that destroyed those cities marked the birth of the most dangerous weapons known to humanity. One blast hit Hiroshima with a force equal to fifteen thousand tons of conventional explosive, while the Nagasaki strike equaled twenty-one thousand tons. The immediate death toll from the two blasts topped one hundred thousand, not including those who died later from radiation and its effects. President Truman had ended the war at a horrible cost, but defended his order on the grounds that even more lives would have been lost if the war had continued.

Not everyone supported Truman's decision to use the atomic bomb. Pacifists hoped anger about the bomb would trigger a revival of peace movements, such as those that followed World War I. But the fear and suspicion engendered by World War II would have more lasting effects—the United States and Russia had barely emerged as victorious allies before they turned against one another.

Winston Churchill, the British leader who had helped unite America with England against Hitler, warned that Russian Communism was as great a danger to democ-

This photograph shows the mushroom cloud from the atomic bomb's explosion over Hiroshima on August 6, 1945. The bomb, along with the one dropped on Nagasaki, unleashed the most destructive force humankind had ever wielded.

racy as Nazism. Truman declared a policy calling for the United States to help free nations throughout the world resist communist aggression, and he portrayed this fight as a struggle against evil. In 1949, Russia detonated its first atomic bomb. Russian and U.S. delegates quarreled angrily on the floor of the United Nations. Popular sentiment in America supported maintaining a nuclear arsenal to be used as a deterrent against Russia. Tensions were so high that the American pacifist movement began to be regarded as subversive.

Adverse public opinion had never deterred the Fellowship of Reconciliation, however. FOR director A. J. Muste and Bayard Rustin believed just as strongly as ever in their cause. Rustin was back on the road again within two weeks of his parole, preaching nonviolence as a means to combat racial discrimination. He not only lectured about combating racism but also resisted segregation almost everywhere he encountered it.

Even where Jim Crow laws were not enforced, some businesses took it on themselves to deny service to African Americans. When denied a hotel reservation at the Hamline Hotel in Saint Paul, Minnesota, Rustin contacted the NAACP, which rallied supporters in the lobby. When the hotel relented and offered him a room, Rustin chose instead to stay at the home of one of those who had protested on his behalf.

The FOR wanted to use Rustin's considerable talents to support Mahatma Gandhi's continuing efforts to free India from British rule. In 1946, the fellowship established a Free India Committee, with Rustin as its chairperson. He spoke against Britain's colonization of India and took part in sit-in protests at the British Embassy in Washington. He greatly desired to meet Gandhi, but travel to India would have to wait. The battle against Jim Crow entered a crucial phase in June of 1946, when the U.S. Supreme Court issued a landmark ruling on segregated trains and buses.

The case stemmed from an incident that occurred in July of 1944, while Rustin was still in the penitentiary. An African-American woman named Irene Morgan, recovering from recent surgery, got on a Greyhound bus in Gloucester County, Virginia. Still feeling weak from the operation, she took a seat at the front of the bus in the white section. The driver ordered her to the back, but she refused to budge. She was arrested at a stop in Saluda, North Carolina. Her case attracted the attention of the NAACP, which decided to test it at the highest levels of the federal court.

In *Morgan v. Virginia,* the Supreme Court handed Irene Morgan and her NAACP lawyers a victory. The decision in her favor rested on the fact that she was riding an interstate bus—one that crossed the border between Virginia and North Carolina. The ruling therefore only dealt with a narrow portion of segregation. Still, the court knocked a small crack in the foundation of Jim Crow when it decided in Morgan's favor. The justices ruled that forcing passengers to change seats when they crossed state lines was unduly burdensome and unconstitutional, so interstate buses could not be segregated.

But as the organizers of FOR and CORE knew, there could be a great gap between the law and everyday practice in the United States, particularly the South. Rustin and George Houser, who shared the job of being FOR's race relations secretary, began planning a series of bus rides by white and black activists into the upper South—Virginia, North Carolina, Tennessee, and Kentucky. Black riders would take seats in the front sections of buses, while white riders would sit in the back. The experiment would be known as the Journey of Reconciliation.

Sixteen riders departed from Washington on the morning of April 9, 1947. They planned stops in fifteen cities, with thirty speaking engagements to explain their mission at churches, colleges, and NAACP meetings. The NAACP had promised legal assistance in the event of arrests. Rustin and Houser had thoroughly schooled the riders in the techniques of nonviolent resistance.

A ride from Richmond to Petersburg, Virginia, went without incident, but a black man warned two of the riders of the risk they were taking. They might get away with challenging Jim Crow in Virginia, the man said, but "the farther South you go, the crazier they get."

At Oxford, North Carolina, the driver called the police, but the officers refused to make an arrest. Nerves frayed, however, during the forty-five minute delay. A middle-aged black teacher begged Rustin to move. "Please move," he said. "Don't do this. You'll reach your destination either in front or in back. What difference does it make?" Rustin explained the mission of the riders. When the bus arrived in Durham, the teacher again sought Rustin's cooperation, this time to keep his name out of any publicity the riders received. "It will hurt me in the community," the man explained.

African-American passengers frequently urged the Journey of Reconciliation riders either to get off the buses or to move to the back. On a Trailways bus from Petersburg, Virginia, to Raleigh, North Carolina, a bus driver called the police to arrest Conrad Lynn, a black civil rights attorney. He apologized to Lynn, but explained that he had to follow orders from the bus company. A black porter boarding the bus was considerably

Members of the 1947 Journey of Reconciliation. *Left to right:* Worth Randle, Wallace Nelson, Ernest Bromley, James Peck, Igal Roodenko, Bayard Rustin, James Felmet, George Houser, and Andrew Johnson. *(Bayard Rustin Estate)*

more hostile. He looked at Lynn and said "What's the matter with him? He's crazy. Where does he think he is? We know how to deal with him. We ought to drag him off."

Rustin saw those African Americans who urged the riders to comply with segregated seating as similar to lower-class Indians who supported the caste system, a system built on rigid class distinctions: "Their request was either the result of fear or, as in the case of the Negro porter, an attempt to ingratiate themselves with white authorities," he reported. "Such reactions are to be expected in a caste system and represent the kind of personal degradation which ought to spur us on to eliminate caste."

Among blacks, the least supportive were the well-to-do who had succeeded despite discrimination, such as the group in Durham, North Carolina, who urged the NAACP to cancel a Reconciliation meeting planned at a church there. These were not the people who rode buses in the first place, according to one of the riders. "Whenever they emerge from their prosperous homes, they ride in cars," he reported. "These people . . . opposed our journey, as many prosperous Negroes oppose action which threatens their privileged status."

Resentment boiled over into violence when the group reached Chapel Hill, North Carolina. Their arrival in town began peacefully enough. They met with supporters in the home of Reverend Charles Jones, the clergyman at Chapel Hill Presbyterian Church. Jones had known Rustin for a long time and had served on the national council of FOR. In the afternoon, the group prepared to board the bus for Greensboro.

The police were waiting for them. No sooner had they taken their seats than they were yanked up, taken from the bus, and arrested. Rustin was among the group of four taken into custody. A group of cab drivers milling around outside the bus station gathered to watch the arrest. The incident sparked their interest, and when word spread of the reasons for the arrest, the ugly face of mob violence emerged.

As the police escorted Rustin and the other men to jail, the taxi drivers surrounded the bus. Journalist James Peck got off the bus to post bail for those arrested and found himself in a circle of five cab drivers. "Coming down here to stir up the niggers," one of the drivers said, and punched Peck in the head with his fist. Two people, one white and one black, rebuked the cab driver, but were told to mind their own business. The mood at the police station was ominous. "They'll never get a bus out of here tonight," someone said, and word spread that the riders might be in serious danger.

Bond was set at fifty dollars each. Reverend Jones drove the men to his home as two cabs filled with taxi drivers followed. When Jones reached his house, the cabs stopped, too. Men jumped out, grabbing sticks and rocks. They began to charge Jones's house, but one among them called them back and they faded away. Shortly thereafter, the phone rang. "Get those damn niggers out of town," the anonymous caller threatened, "or we'll burn your house down. We'll be around to see that they go."

By this time, getting the riders out of Chapel Hill alive was the only thing that mattered to Jones and the other supporters. Two cars drove them the fifty miles to Greensboro, the next scheduled stop on the Reconciliation ride.

The incident in Chapel Hill marked the high tide of violent threats against the Reconciliation activists. For the rest of the journey, they met with the same mixed reactions they had in the beginning. Some people, white and black, grumbled about their crossing of the color line, while others accepted it. One driver might have the riders arrested, while the next ignored them. By the end of the Reconciliation ride, two weeks after it began, police had carried out arrests on six occasions, with a total of twelve riders charged.

Remarkably, the police made every arrest without violence. This stood in contrast to Rustin's earlier ordeal in Tennessee, when Nashville officers had beat him savagely. He concluded that a group of determined protesters could avoid violence by applying Gandhi's principles of nonviolence. "Without exception those arrested behaved in a nonviolent fashion," he wrote. "They acted without fear, spoke quietly and firmly, showing great consideration for the police and bus drivers, and repeatedly pointed to the fact that they expected the police to do their duty as they saw it. We cannot overemphasize the necessity for this courteous and intelligent conduct while breaking with the caste system. We believe that the reason the police behaved politely was that there was not the slightest provocation in the attitude of the resisters."

Rustin saw the ride as a vindication of using nonviolent means to protest racial injustice. The mob in Chapel Hill had been frightening, but considering the decades of lynching, burning, and other violence directed against African Americans, it was remarkable to have violated Jim Crow without bloodshed. In twenty-six violations of segregated seating practices, only one punch had been thrown. "We are of the opinion that in most cases if the bus drivers had not taken action, the passengers would have continued to ignore the Negroes sitting in the front of a bus or in coaches for whites," Rustin wrote. "Between Statesville and Asheville, North Carolina, a clear statement from the driver explaining the Morgan decision [the recent Supreme Court ruling] quieted protesting white passengers."

Rustin felt elated at the project's conclusion, as did most of the other activists. They felt they had knocked at least a small hole into the old wall of racism in the South. Though Rustin and several other riders still faced charges, they felt confident that the NAACP would overturn the convictions or get the penalties reduced to minimal fines.

A North Carolina judge, however, gave those arrested in Chapel Hill their first taste of the trouble ahead. Rustin and Andrew Johnson, a black law student, were sentenced to thirty days each on a chain gang. Their two white counterparts drew stiffer sentences of ninety days each. Judge Henry Whitfield explained his reasoning to Rustin and Igal Roodenko, a former conscientious objector who happened to be white.

Rustin recalled, "He said to me, 'Well, I know you're a poor misled nigra from the North. Therefore, I'm going to give you thirty days.' Then, very angrily, he said 'Now, Mr. Rodenky'—purposely mispronouncing Roodenko's name—'I presume you're Jewish, Mr. Rodenky.' Igal said 'Yes, I'm Jewish.' The judge said 'Well, it's about time you Jews from New York learned that you can't come down here bringing your nigras with you to upset the customs of the South. Just to teach you a lesson, I gave your black boy thirty days, now I give you ninety.'"

The NAACP immediately appealed the sentences. Bayard continued his work for FOR and CORE, confident that he could build on the success of the Journey of Reconciliation. But the defense of Rustin and the other riders hit a snag shortly after the verdict from Judge Whitfield. The NAACP gave the interstate bus tickets, a vital piece of defense evidence, to an attorney in Durham, North Carolina. To this day it remains unclear exactly what that lawyer did with those tickets and why, but there is no mistaking the fact that they disappeared while in his possession.

Seven

Chain Gang

The Journey of Reconciliation ended in a glow of triumph. The bus riders were confident that they had publicly exposed Jim Crow and segregation for the evils they were. Their work on the Journey earned Bayard Rustin and fellow FOR secretary George Houser the Thomas Jefferson Award for the Advancement of Democracy from the Council Against Intolerance in America. In April of 1948, they were honored at a banquet at the Waldorf-Astoria hotel in New York. Neither was aware that the painful cost of the journey had yet to be fully paid.

In his speech to the council, Rustin said the fight against discrimination could not end with the integration of buses and stressed the importance of desegregating the military. "While there is a very real question whether any army can bring freedom, certainly a Jim Crow army cannot," he said. "On the contrary, to those it attempts to liberate, it will bring discrimination and segregation such as we are now exporting to Europe and to South America. . . . Segregation in the military must be resisted if democracy and peace are to survive."

Rustin had joined A. Philip Randolph's Committee Against Jim Crow in Military Service and Training. Randolph had formed the committee after President Harry Truman's administration introduced a bill for Universal Military Training, a program requiring every young man to receive a year of military training— African Americans as well as whites. The program did not discriminate, but the military still practiced segregation and assigned the most menial tasks to black men.

Randolph said publicly and in front of Congress that he would counsel black men to refuse to obey the law if it passed. One congressman warned him that such counsel would amount to treason. Randolph said he would risk such a charge for the "soul" of the nation.

"I believe that is the price we have to pay for the democracy we want," Randolph said, and went on, "I would be willing to face that [charge] on the theory and on the grounds that we are serving a higher law than the law which applies the act of treason to us when we are attempting to win democracy. . . . We would participate in no overt acts against our government. Ours would be one of non-participation in the military forces of the country. We would be willing to absorb the violence, to

absorb the terror-
ism, to face the
music and take
whatever comes."

The Universal
Military Training
Act passed despite
Randolph's objec-
tions. Randolph
then issued an ulti-
matum to President
Truman, promising
that African Ameri-
cans would defy the
draft if Truman did
not prohibit dis-
crimination in the
military. Randolph

President Truman eventually capitulated to
Randolph's demands for equal treatment of African
Americans in the military.

was then the country's most prominent black leader. If
Truman ignored Randolph, he risked losing black votes—
and 1948 was an election year.

Randolph set up the League for Nonviolent Civil
Disobedience, a group that would defy the law if necessary. Bayard Rustin, James Peck, and George Houser,
all former Journey of Reconciliation riders, helped him
organize. Rustin served as field director for the League.
In July, A. Philip Randolph addressed a rally in front of
the Theresa Hotel. FBI agents roamed the crowd. A
member of the audience asked Randolph what he ex-

pected them to do about the new law. "My answer is this," he answered. "You should not register under this draft act."

Randolph could have been arrested for urging men to resist the draft. His reputation, however, offered him a shield. None of the agents or their superiors wanted the newspapers to carry pictures of them escorting America's best-known African-American leader away in handcuffs.

Nor did President Truman want a racial controversy to explode with the election only months away. Just as President Roosevelt had done, Truman finally buckled under the pressure of Randolph's organized defiance. On July 26, he issued Executive Order 9981, which stated that "there shall be equality of treatment and opportunity for all persons in the armed services, without regard to race, color, religion, or national origin." In exchange, Randolph planned to dismantle the League for Nonviolent Civil Disobedience.

Randolph saw Truman's order as a great triumph and a vindication of the struggle for equal rights. Some of his younger colleagues, including Rustin, did not share his enthusiasm. They were unhappy that the order did not ban segregation, just unequal treatment. They urged Randolph to reconsider disbanding the league. Rustin and William Sutherland, another league leader, argued that the group should stay active until the military erased all discrimination, including segregation, from its ranks. Randolph was determined to honor his word. He ordered Rustin and Sutherland to set up a press conference at which he would announce the group had been dissolved.

The two young men used their knowledge of the press to ambush the elder activist. At that time, most city newspapers published morning and afternoon editions, often under different mastheads. Rustin and Sutherland scheduled Randolph's press conference for 4 PM, then called a separate conference for the morning.

The leaders of the League for Nonviolent Civil Disobedience announced their disagreement with Randolph's decision. They told a room full of reporters that they were "morally bound to continue the civil disobedience campaign until the object for which the League is organized is accomplished." When Randolph arrived for his afternoon press conference, he found a sparse crowd. The afternoon papers had already run with the story, and the headlines were not what he had planned. The reporters wrote about dissension in the civil rights movement rather than its success in forcing the U.S. president to change military policy.

Later in his life, Bayard would warn young radicals not to defeat themselves. Over time, that is just what he began to feel he and Sutherland had done by hijacking Randolph's press conference. He felt ashamed. It was two years before he could even face Randolph again.

Rustin had planned to travel abroad to meet with members of the Indian resistance movement, but had postponed his trip to work on Randolph's campaign. The rift he had created with his mentor made a trip away from New York all the more desirable, since he did not want to face Randolph. The American Friends Service Committee

The *Queen Mary,* the ship that carried Rustin abroad.

named Rustin as its delegate to an international pacifist conference. In October of 1948, he boarded the *Queen Mary,* bound first for England, then for India.

Rustin was enchanted when he saw London for the first time. Though German bombers had razed large sections of the city, leaving rubble, ruins, and pitted roads in once thriving neighborhoods, London still held enormous appeal. Rustin loved to browse the antique shops, seeking out old musical instruments to add to his collection. While in London, he learned that the pacifist conference had been cancelled, but FOR allowed him to make his journey to India anyway.

There he had hoped to meet Mahatma Gandhi, but tragedy denied him the chance. Ten months before Rustin's trip, on January 30, 1948, a Hindu enraged by Gandhi's campaign to reconcile Hindus and Muslims shot Gandhi to death. Rustin and millions around the world were devastated by the violent act.

Rustin in India in 1948 with Muriel Lester, the International FOR's traveling secretary and a friend of Gandhi's. *(Fellowship of Reconciliation)*

Muriel Lester, an English ambassador for the Fellowship of Reconciliation, helped Bayard meet many other influential leaders, including Gandhi's son Devadas and India's prime minister, Jawaharlal Nehru.

Always persuasive and charming, Bayard made a particularly strong impression on Indian audiences. He dropped his Western manner of dress, and began to wear plain white calico garments and sandals. He adopted the Indian style of greeting, bowing from the waist with his fingers together and pointed upward. He learned to greet Indians in their own language and eat while seated with his legs crossed under him. Indian journalists began to seek interviews with him as though he were an official ambassador.

When it came time for him to return to America,

Lester pleaded with Muste to extend Rustin's stay. She wrote that his effectiveness was "three times as much [as that] of a white pacifist," adding that it was "a perfect example of God's providence" that he had come to India. But Muste insisted on Bayard's return, saying that FOR needed his talents at home.

Rustin had another reason to return to the United States. The NAACP had exhausted its efforts to overturn his sentence for violating Jim Crow laws in North Carolina. In January 1949, Rustin began his journey home, knowing he was facing time on a state chain gang. It was an unhappy departure from a land where he had been treated as a leader of the global peace movement.

Late in the afternoon of March 21, 1949, Bayard surrendered to the Orange County court in Hillsborough, North Carolina. He sat alone in his small cell, expecting the sparse supper of an inmate. But he was not even fed that night. Later he found that men on the chain gang had only two meals a day: breakfast at seven o'clock in the morning and lunch at noon.

At two o'clock the following afternoon, guards put Bayard and another prisoner into a "dog car"—a small truck with a locked screen in the rear. They traveled an hour through the rain until Bayard got his first look at the place that would be his home for the duration of his sentence. It was a long low building surrounded by barbed wire. Only sparse grass sprouted along the grounds. There were no trees. The inside was no less dismal. Mud caked the floor, roaches ran everywhere, and there was not so much as a box for a prisoner to keep his possessions.

A prison barber shaved Rustin's head. A guard took him to a dormitory with bunk beds crowded so close that men had to walk sideways to get to them. The stark lights in the room stayed on all night. The bell calling the men to work rang at five-thirty the next morning. Bayard began his first chain-gang shift—ten hours of roadwork, half an hour for lunch. He worked in a crew of fifteen men, herded by a "walking boss" and under the watch of a guard with a revolver and a shotgun.

"I started from the camp for my first day's work on the road with anything but an easy mind," Rustin later wrote. When they first got off the truck, the guards let the men stand for several moments in silence.

"Hey, you, tall boy!" the walking guard asked Rustin. "How much time you got?" Rustin replied that he had been sentenced to thirty days. The guard took a newspaper clipping from his pocket, one about Rustin's rides with the Journey of Reconciliation.

"You're the one who thinks he's smart," the man said, his face growing red with anger. "Ain't got no respect. Tries to be uppity. Well, we'll learn you. You'll learn you got to respect us down here. You ain't in Yankeeland now. We don't like no Yankee ways." He punctuated his threat with a blow, striking not Rustin, but the man to his left.

The walking guard shoved a pick into Rustin's hands. He had never used a pick on hard ground before, and learned in short order how backbreaking the labor was. He chopped with the tool for about ten minutes, then felt the strength begin to ebb from his arms and back.

Chain gang guards would club prisoners with gun butts for the slightest infractions and beat them with leather straps. The most extreme punishment was being hung by one's wrists by the bars, facing the cell. After a

This painting by Harlem Renaissance artist William Johnson captures some of the exhaustion and endlessness that characterized life on a chain gang. *(Courtesy of the Smithsonian American Art Museum, Washington, D.C. / Art Resource.)*

few hours, this torture caused the feet and groin to swell.

Rustin saw the ordeal as designed not just to punish the prisoners, but to break their spirit and make them feel less than human. Despite their cruelty, Bayard tried to keep himself from hating the guards. He took every opportunity to stand the system on its head by talking with them, forcing them to see him as a person.

"I wanted to work hard so I would not be a burden to other chain-gangers," he wrote. "I wanted to accept the imprisonment in a quiet, unobtrusive manner. Only in this way, I believed, could the officials and guards be led to consider sympathetically the principle on which I was convicted. I did not expect them to agree with me, but I did want them to believe I cared enough about the ideals I was supposed to stand for so I could accept my punishment with a sense of humor, fairness, and con-structive good will [sic]."

One day while Bayard was struggling to make cement pipe, he saw the walking guard approaching him with a hostile look. He had noticed that the man was skilled in construction trades and decided to use his own poor skills as an excuse to create a dialogue.

"Captain Jones, I seem to need help," he said. "Would you have the time to show . . ." The guard cut him off in mid-sentence. "Damn well you need help," he said. But Rustin noticed the hostility fade from the man's face as he explained how to scrape and oil the steel forms. Rustin thanked him for the lesson, and said he would be grateful for any more. An hour later, the man returned and looked with satisfaction at Rustin's progress.

"Well, Rusty, you're learnin'," he said. It was the first time that the guard had called him a name other than "boy" or "hey, you." He later gave Rustin cigarettes, which Rustin passed on to another inmate.

Such results encouraged Rustin, but he did not deceive himself into thinking that he was making profound changes in racist thinking or the prison system. Unlike most prisoners, he had a good education, influence, and powerful friends on the outside. He felt his attempts to influence the guards amounted only to a small step.

Rustin was released on good behavior after serving twenty-two days. Before leaving the state, he traveled to Chapel Hill to speak at the University of North Carolina. He told about his ordeals and those of others, so persuasively indicting the state's chain gang system that the faculty formed a committee to protest to Governor Kerr Scott. He wrote a report on his experiences that was published by the *New York Post* and the *Baltimore Afro-American,* and was widely read in both the North and the South.

Thousands of prisoners had suffered the tortures of the chain gang in silence. When Rustin's writing and speeches shined a light on the barbarous injustices done to the inmates in chains, things began to change rapidly. In Rockingham, where a Journey of Reconciliation rider was hung on the bars, a guard was convicted of inflicting bodily harm on an inmate. Within two years, North Carolina abolished chain gangs. Bayard Rustin had proven that nonviolence could topple a violent system.

Eight

Exile

Even as Rustin and his colleagues were gaining victories over discrimination and violence, the world around them was becoming more suspicious and dangerous. The tension between communist Russia and the United States continued to increase as each nation worked feverishly to develop and stockpile nuclear weapons. This marked the beginning of what came to be called the cold war—"cold" because there was almost no direct confrontation between the two countries, but each considered the other its enemy and maneuvered to gain more power and influence.

Because Russia was a communist country, most people in the United States quickly came to fear and distrust anyone who advocated communist beliefs. Senator Joseph McCarthy of Wisconsin started a crusade against

This collage combines several of the key symbols of America's fear of communism, often called the "Red Scare." The figure draped in the American flag is Senator Joseph McCarthy.

communism, and, beginning in 1948, chaired a Senate committee that publicized charges against powerful and influential people. Most of these allegations were never proven to be true but they indelibly damaged people's reputations and created an environment of hostility and suspicion. Dissent of any kind became linked with subversion. Two years later, communist North Korea attacked South Korea and the United States sent in troops. Public sentiment about the danger of communism rose to a fevered pitch, and anyone who spoke out in favor of peace was branded a traitor.

Organized street rallies turned dangerous for Bayard Rustin and his cohorts in the Fellowship of Reconciliation. Rustin joined the Peacemakers, a group sponsored by FOR and other pacifist organizations. At a rally in Times Square, a man misread a sign reading "Catholic Worker" (one of the sponsoring groups) as "Daily Worker," a pro-Communist newspaper. He flew into a rage and attacked Peacemaker David Dellinger in the middle of a speech, knocking him out cold. Bayard grabbed a broken picket sign and told the assailant to hit him instead. His anger spent, the man stopped his attacks.

FOR had to pick its campaigns carefully. Some thought they should scale back unpopular protests in the United States in order to concentrate on causes abroad. Various independence movements in Africa attracted the interest of young FOR activists, including struggles in Ghana and Nigeria to throw off British colonial rule. Several FOR officers competed for the chance to travel to Africa. In 1952, Rustin became the first to go.

He stopped first in Accra, Ghana, where he met movement leader Kwame Nkrumah. Nkrumah was the head of the Convention People's Party (CPP), which sought to obtain Ghana's independence from the British. Bayard helped Nkrumah establish a youth group for the CPP. Nkrumah was a hugely popular figure in Ghana. People

Rustin visiting with Kwame Nkrumah in Ghana in 1952. *(Fellowship of Reconciliation)*

raised him to mythical status, claiming he could go without eating, sleeping, or drinking, and that he could make himself invisible. He would later be elected Ghana's first president.

"My experience here has been staggering," Rustin wrote of the city of Accra. "In this dirty, poor, ambitious city, I find much that I find in Harlem. We [African Americans] left here in 1619, yet the people here sing, laugh, walk, cry, dance, and strive in a way that is like 125th Street and Lenox Avenue. I seem to know and understand them as I do nowhere else but in Harlem."

Nkrumah sent praise of Rustin to Nnamdi Azikiwe, who was building a similar independence movement in Nigeria. Azikiwe, called "Zik" by his people, was an affluent businessman who had used his chain of newspapers to spread his anti-colonial message. Rustin took over editorial work one of those papers, *The Pilot*, allowing Azikiwe to spend more time organizing. In 1954, Azikiwe would be elected premier of East Nigeria.

The spirit of change was flourishing in Africa. In 1952, the African National Congress began a campaign against the apartheid rule of South Africa. Upon returning to the States, Rustin took up that cause and helped set up the Committee Against Apartheid in South Africa.

"Apartheid" means "apartness" in Afrikaans, the language established in South Africa by Dutch settlers. Like Jim Crow laws in the American South, apartheid prohibited white and nonwhite people from mixing. Apartheid meant segregated public facilities, segre-

A South African township. Apartheid, like segregation, created a stark contrast between the standards of living in black and white areas.

gated school systems, and even forced relocations to segregated neighborhoods. The Fellowship of Reconciliation committee was the first in America to protest the system in South Africa.

Rustin again toured the United States, this time to raise money for another trip to Africa. In January of 1953, he gave his usual rousing speech, this time at the Pasadena Athletic Club, at a gathering organized by the American Association of University Women. As usual, people crowded around him at the end of his lecture. Newspapers published glowing accounts of his visit.

In the following day's editions, however, many of them would publish his name in their police sections. The night after his speech, the Pasadena police found Rustin and two other men having a sexual encounter in a car. He was arrested and charged with "sex perversion," on the grounds that he had solicited the men for sex. At that time, every state in America had laws on the books that made sodomy illegal. A judge rejected an appeal by Rustin's lawyer to free him on the condition that he leave the state, and sentenced all three men to jail for sixty days.

This charge and subsequent conviction immediately toppled Rustin from his status as one of the most gifted leaders of the Fellowship of Reconciliation. His devotion to social causes had made him highly visible and more vulnerable to scandal. Almost overnight he was an outcast. There was a general sense that Bayard Rustin, a man who stood up for principle, had violated a moral code. According to the standards of the time, he had been disgraced.

Rustin's mentor, A. J. Muste, had long known that Rustin was gay. He had repeatedly counseled Rustin to seek a "cure," and had warned him that his sexuality could hurt FOR's reputation. In Muste's view, an organization that claimed to defend right from wrong could hardly harbor a convicted degenerate. After the Pasadena verdict, Muste had FOR issue a lengthy statement that began "To our great sorrow, Bayard Rustin was convicted on a 'morals charge' and sentenced to 60 days in the Los Angeles County Jail on January 23, 1953. As of that date, and at his own suggestion, his service as an FOR staff member terminated." Newspapers across the country published this news. Muste and other leaders did their best to disassociate themselves from Rustin lest they too be tainted by his crime.

Glenn Smiley, FOR's California representative, visited Rustin at the Roncho Honor prison farm. "Bayard was in tears," Smiley recalled. "He was most repentant over the homosexual incident because of the grief it had brought A. J. Muste." Rustin said later he never felt guilt about being gay, but Muste's anger made him feel he had betrayed the pacifist movement.

In a society that punished homosexuality as a crime, Rustin had learned the value of keeping relationships discrete. There were close-knit gay communities, especially in New York, where a person could feel comfortable and safe. But the nature of Rustin's work, which required him to travel across America, forced him out of the familiar circles of his home city. Alone and out of his element, he had no support system to fall back on, no stalwart group of friends to call to his rescue.

The 1950s was a conservative decade. The civil rights movement survived because it had strength in numbers—people across the country willing to stand, shoulder to shoulder, against discrimination based on skin color. Homosexuals had no such voice. Rustin's activism faltered without the empowerment of a movement behind him. While he was comfortable with his own sexuality, he would have needed the power of the people behind him to fight the judgment of society. Abandoned by his friends and associates, Rustin was isolated and alienated from the world that had once revered him.

Rustin faced the full force of this condemnation when he returned to New York and began seeking work. He had been a professional activist for his entire career. With the taint of arrest for a socially unacceptable behavior, he found it nearly impossible to get any job calling for him to assume a public role. He resorted to applying for menial jobs, even taking work moving furniture. Most employers, however, considered him overqualified for physical labor. He sought help from a social worker, who also found him hard to place. The social worker "suggested that hospitals always need personnel for cleaning jobs, etc., and suggested also the possibility of [Rustin] getting a job as a domestic, that is, as a butler."

Six months after his arrest, the War Resisters League (WRL) came to Bayard's rescue. The WRL had worked closely with the Fellowship of Reconciliation and held similar views. But unlike FOR, the WRL had no connection to any religion. A socialist teacher named Jesse Wallace Hughan had founded the group in the 1920s. Young radicals dominated the league. They admired Rustin's work for FOR, and decided to hire him despite the Pasadena scandal. "We said 'We can get him now,' for we had always begrudged his outstanding work for the Fellowship," recalled Igal Roodenko, WRL member and former Reconciliation rider. Bayard was appointed executive director of the War Resisters League in the summer of 1953.

Rustin worked for the WRL for twelve years. He helped them expand their activities beyond pacifism into the civil rights movement and the international struggle against colonial rule in Africa. He went back to Africa as the WRL spokesman, and helped leaders such as Kenneth Kaunda of Zambia and Julius Nyerere of Tanzania in their battles for national independence.

Still, Rustin continued to face challenges from some of his former allies. In 1954, the American Friends Service Committee (AFSC) sought to gather intellectuals for a convention. The AFSC wanted to write a document that summed up current pacifist beliefs. But when Stephen Cary, an AFSC staff officer, submitted his list of candidates, they asked that Rustin's name be removed.

"They were embarrassed by his homosexuality, which became public knowledge after the matter in California," Cary reported. "But I resisted. I told them I didn't give a damn what Bayard was. . . . I wasn't going to write him off my list." So when the group convened at Haverford College, Rustin was among its members.

Rustin took a role that he had honed in his years with FOR, stepping in to help bickering members reconcile opposing views. For more than a week, the group hammered away at its mission, often working late into the night. They produced a document called *Speak Truth to Power.* Its authors challenged many of the assumptions of the time, arguing that the obsession with military might was undermining American democracy. They charged that Americans had become so obsessed with fighting communists that they had become like them, enforcing conformity and repressing free speech. They advocated nonviolence as a principle of social change.

Speak Truth to Power was published in both magazine and book form and sparked debate in the United States and abroad. Stephen Cary said the work could never have been written without Rustin's help.

Yet when the time came to assign authorship for the work, Bayard asked that his name be left off. He reminded the group of his Pasadena arrest and said that his name among the authors would hurt the document's circulation. Cary urged him to reconsider. Bayard declined. As the group prepared to disperse from the campus, he sang two moving spirituals to them: "There Is a Balm in Gilead" and "Nobody Knows the Trouble I've Seen."

"The effect was overwhelming," Cary recalled. "And then he said, 'Gentlemen, I'm at peace. It's been a wonderful week. Just leave my name off.' Especially after that week, I was never able to assign a moral dimension to people's sexuality."

Bayard became increasingly bound by the stigma of being gay. The WRL had saved his career, and he would repay it by helping accomplish work that would change America. Only rarely, however, would he share the prestige. In coming to terms with his homosexuality, Rustin had to accept the contradiction of being both an activist and an invisible man.

Nine

Mission to Montgomery

In May of 1954, the United States Supreme Court issued its ruling in the famous *Brown v. Board of Education* case. The court unanimously agreed that segregated education was not constitutional—not even under the guise of the separate-but-equal doctrine. More than half a century of experience had proven that black schools would never get equal treatment. From then on, all schools would have to admit white and black students.

The ruling set off a panic. The Ku Klux Klan, responsible for uncounted lynchings and other terrorism, raised the level of its threats and intimidation. Almost as bad were the White Citizens' Councils, which tried to crush integration through economic means. The Councils often published tracts filled with racial epithets that would have been worthy of the Klan. But they mainly used

Norman Rockwell's painting *The Problem We All Live With* was inspired by the story of young Ruby Bridges, one of the first African Americans to attend a white school. *(Reproduced by permission of the Norman Rockwell Family Agency, Inc.)*

financial intimidation, denying African Americans credit to start businesses, forcing black tenants from rented homes, or getting them fired from their jobs. The Councils, as Rustin put it, were the "Ku Klux Klan in gray flannel suits."

Rustin helped form In Friendship, a group dedicated to providing aid to African Americans fighting discrimination in the South. Ella Baker, an influential field secretary for the NAACP, provided a list of Southern contacts that would aid the fledgling organization. In Friendship's early members also included Stanley Levison, a wealthy real estate lawyer active in the American Jewish Congress (AJC). The AJC and other civil rights groups often cooperated with each other, believing they all fought a common enemy in discrimination and injustice. A. Philip Randolph, Bayard's old mentor, helped Rustin, Baker, and Levison make contacts with unions. Levison's activism attracted the support of other groups, including the Jewish Labor Committee.

In Friendship's main goal was to provide activists with the money they so desperately needed. It paid the rent for people who had been kicked out of their houses for supporting integration and funded farmers with canceled credit. Just as In Friendship was beginning its financial aid campaign, an event in Montgomery, Alabama, thrust the campaign onto the center stage of the national news. On December 1, 1955, Rosa Parks famously refused to move to the back of the bus.

Parks, a seamstress and worker for the local NAACP, had suffered abuse at the hands of white bus drivers in the past, once being ordered off by an enraged driver after she violated the seating patterns. On that winter day in 1955, she took her seat as usual in the front row of the "colored" section. As the bus filled up, the driver noticed white people were standing and ordered Parks to give up her seat. She refused. She was arrested for violating the law requiring segregated seating on buses.

Southern anti-segregation groups, including the Women's Political Council, had been working to challenge the laws since the 1940s. Dr. Mary Fair Burks had founded the WPC in 1946, partly because the League of Women Voters refused to accept African-American women. Most of the black people who rode the buses were women, since it was not considered appropriate for them to hitchhike or walk long distances as the men did. Six months before Parks was arrested, the women of the

WPC had written to the mayor asking for fairer treatment on the bus lines.

Rosa Parks was an appealing defendant for the NAACP's case. She was a hard-working woman with no arrest record, an upright citizen with a job. With her neat

This sculpture by Marshall D. Rumbaugh depicts the arrest of Rosa Parks. *(Courtesy of the National Portrait Gallery, Smithsonian Institution / Art Resource.)*

bun and spectacles, she presented an unexpected image for an agitator.

Parks did not refuse to give up her seat simply because she was too tired from a hard day's work to stand, as some newspapers first reported. She had sought for much of her adult life to resist injustice, which led her to work for the NAACP. Her grandmother had been a slave and told her of the evils of a system that allowed some people to be owned by others.

As a child, Parks's grandmother had to take her dinner from a large pot placed in the yard, where food for slaves was poured like slop for pigs. Her grandfather, though crippled, was made to go barefoot and was severely beaten by overseers. Parks attended a seminar at Highlander Folk School in Tennessee, where she lived in an integrated environment and was schooled on social activism. Highlander was initially founded to address the problems of oppressed workers in the Appalachian Mountains, but evolved into a training ground for civil rights workers as well. After working side by side with whites at Highlander, Parks found it even harder to endure the indignity of segregation: "It was a struggle—I don't know if you could call it that—just to be human, to be a citizen, to have the rights and privileges of any other person."

Four days after Parks's arrest, black leaders formed the Montgomery Improvement Association (MIA) to push for an end to bus discrimination. The Association launched a boycott, calling for all riders to refuse to board buses until they were integrated. Boycotts were illegal in Alabama, but most blacks—and some whites—heeded the call of MIA leaders to stay off the buses. Meanwhile, E. D. Nixon, a longtime organizer for Randolph's Brotherhood of Sleeping Car Porters, sought a charismatic leader to take on the difficult and dangerous job of leading the boycott.

At Dexter Avenue Baptist Church, Nixon had listened to the sermons of a young minister he thought could inspire people. Dr. Martin Luther King Jr. was twenty-six at the time and a newcomer to Montgomery. King had read Gandhi's writings at Boston University and understood nonviolence, at least in theory. But he had no aspirations to lead a civil rights movement. Nixon and other MIA leaders would not take no for an answer, though, and King eventually accepted the role. He would quickly pay the price. The police targeted him for frivolous traffic violations, and in late January, a bomb exploded at his house. A few days later, someone tossed another bomb at Nixon's house.

As people in Montgomery faced serious violence, the leaders of In Friendship decided they had to act. They chose to send Rustin to council King in nonviolent resistance. They had heard that boycott supporters were stocking up on weapons, a seriously misguided approach in the group's opinion. If the Montgomery Improvement Association got into a shootout with racists like those in the Klan, they would stand no chance, and would lose their movement in the riptide of violence.

Montgomery looked like a city at war by the time Rustin arrived. He first met not with King but with Reverend Ralph Abernathy, another MIA leader. Abernathy assured him that MIA was ready to embrace nonviolence, but that sentiment contrasted with what Rustin saw in the streets. Taking a walk outside his hotel one night, he saw guards of black men bristling with guns formed into units to watch the houses of Nixon and King.

When he arrived at King's house, Rustin was warmly welcomed by King's wife, Coretta Scott King. In the 1940s, Rustin had lectured at her high school. She waved aside his letter of introduction and invited him in. "Bayard told me how strongly he felt about our work and the possibility of its developing into a nonviolent move-ment all over the country," she said. "He also spoke of his admiration for my husband. When Martin came home, though they had never met before, they had a wonderful talk [in which] Bayard offered to help in any way he could."

Rustin, then forty-four, provided mature counsel for King, much as Randolph and Muste had done for him. First, there was the matter of weapons. When Rustin saw a gun resting on an armchair in the Kings' living room, he explained why nonviolent leaders should never use firearms. "If in the heat and flow of battle a leader's house is bombed and he shoots back," Rustin recalled explaining, "then that is an encouragement to his fol-lowers to use guns. If, on the other hand, he has no guns

Abernathy, King, and Rustin in Montgomery, February 1956. *(AP Wide World)*

around him, and his followers know it, then they will rise to the nonviolent occasion."

King believed people could be motivated to do good things if the choices of right and wrong were laid out clearly before them. So did Rustin. He congratulated King on a particularly powerful sermon he had given at his Dexter Avenue church. King had preached that racists "should not be hated," because the "most prejudiced mind in Montgomery, in America," could become a "mind of goodwill."

Bayard agreed, but he had seen troubling signs of hate since arriving in Montgomery. One particularly offensive tract distributed by one of the Citizens' Councils declared that "all whites are created equal with certain rights; among these are life, liberty, and the pursuit of dead niggers."

"I cannot believe that this leaflet reflects the thinking of all white people in Montgomery," Rustin wrote. "Thousands of them would no doubt be nauseated by it. Yet I report its distribution because such hate literature . . . is an aspect of the emotional climate in which grave problems must be solved."

In the meantime, the courts quickly made use of the state's antiboycott law to suppress the fledgling movement in Montgomery. Just before Rustin arrived, King and almost one hundred other MIA members were indicted for organizing the protest. Rather than resist arrest, Rustin urged them to surrender. Gandhi's followers had used just such a tactic, and being arrested lost its stigma in his movement. The civil rights leaders followed Rustin's advice.

"White community leaders, politicians, and police were flabbergasted," Rustin said. "Negroes were thrilled to see their leaders surrender without being hunted down."

Rustin helped draft some of King's speeches and wrote the first article to appear under his name, a piece called "Our Struggle" that was published in *Liberation* magazine. The two men made a striking contrast on the rare occasions they appeared together publicly. Eighteen years older than King, Rustin was tall, patrician, with elegant gestures and speech. The young King was shorter, with a blocky build, also well spoken, but with a full-blown, ringing speaking style ideal for the pulpit. Rustin's role model was Gandhi, while King's was Christ. The Christian and Gandhian approaches would blend perfectly to define the civil rights movement.

Both were gifted public speakers, but King's ringing oratorical style carried the sound of a Bible read aloud, even when he was talking about contemporary problems, a style that resonated in the ears of his Southern congregations, and would do so as well before national audiences. In one speech, King sought to assure the boycotters that they were in the right to protest, even when the highest authorities stood against them. "And we are not wrong; we are not wrong in what we are doing," he thundered. "If we are wrong, the Supreme Court of this nation is wrong. If we are wrong, the Constitution of the United States is wrong. If we are wrong, Jesus of Nazareth was merely a Utopian dreamer and never came down to earth. If we are wrong, justice

is a lie." The deafening applause shook the church, and a wave of excitement spread even to those who stood outside.

As the boycott stretched into months, the buses lost money. Despite much hardship, people refused to ride. They found ways to

Martin Luther King delivering a speech. *(Library of Congress)*

carpool or friends to walk with.

King's status as a leader grew as the boycotters refused to meet violence with violence. Newspapers printed his eloquent appeals for justice, and money began to pour into the coffers of the Montgomery Improvement Association.

MIA bought vans to transport boycotters. White businesses countered by refusing to insure the vehicles. Lloyd's of London stepped into the gap and provided insurance. Pressure mounted on the authorities to seek an end to the standoff. All but the most die-hard racists could see that the divide between white and blacks was hurting the whole city.

The U.S. Supreme Court finally brought an end to the crisis with its historic ruling of November 13, 1956, declaring that segregation on buses was unconstitutional. MIA waited until the official papers arrived in Montgomery before declaring the boycott at an end. When King, Nixon, and other MIA leaders rode the first integrated bus in Montgomery, Rustin shared no part in the honor. In keeping with his position as a man behind the scenes, he had already flown back to New York. He took the most pride in introducing the principles of nonviolent resistance to the boycott: "Not one of the Negro leaders in Montgomery was a pacifist when the struggle began," he said.

After the victory in Montgomery, both King and the leaders of In Friendship wanted to sustain the momentum of the civil rights movement. They had gained the nation's attention and saw an opportunity unmatched in the history of American race relations. From their desire to create a permanent movement came the Southern Christian Leadership Conference (SCLC).

"I . . . felt that a victory at Montgomery would have no permanent meaning in the racial struggle unless it led to the achievement of dozens of similar victories in the South," Rustin wrote. Ella Baker viewed the new organization as a way to expand the struggle for civil rights beyond the NAACP, which preferred to concentrate its efforts on winning court battles. Stanley Levison wanted a group that could become a national movement.

The In Friendship organizers would have preferred to keep "Christian" out of the name of the conference. Many Jews had worked to end racial discrimination and there was a growing group of black Muslims who might feel excluded. But King refused to concede. In Friendship gave in to King's wishes, and Rustin later admitted that having "Christian" in the name did not appear to alienate non-Christians.

Despite some internal conflicts, the SCLC presented a unified front to the media and the public. It adopted marches as one of its main tools in pushing for change. The tactic could not have suited Rustin better. He remembered the marches on Washington that Randolph had cancelled after gaining concessions from Presidents Roosevelt and Truman. He believed they could still prove effective.

The first such event the SCLC organized was the Prayer Pilgrimage. On February 14, 1957, one day after being elected president of SCLC, King telegraphed President Eisenhower to ask for help: "If you, our President, cannot come South to relieve our harassed people, we shall have to lead our people to you."

Eisenhower did not reply. Rustin set about organizing the march from the NAACP headquarters in New York, with the event to be billed as a joint venture between the two groups. The march was set for the third anniversary of the Supreme Court decision that struck down school segregation, a ruling that still created bitter controversy.

The main goal of the march was to urge President Eisenhower and Congress to speed up the process of school desegregation ordered by the Supreme Court. Organizers also sought to call attention to violence against civil rights activists in the South, attract support in the North, and get more comprehensive legislation passed against racial discrimination. King wanted a bill that would allow the Justice Department to file lawsuits against election boards that denied voting rights to African Americans.

The Pilgrimage drew thirty thousand people to the Lincoln Memorial on May 17, 1957. Bayard and other organizers had hoped for more, but it was still the largest civil rights march ever held in Washington. Celebrities who joined the event helped it attract greater news coverage. Hollywood actors Sidney Poitier and Sammy Davis Jr. came, as did singers Harry Belafonte and Paul Robeson, and the novelist John Oliver Killens.

The Prayer Pilgrimage's achievements were modest in light of the SCLC's goals, but Rustin considered the march an important step for the movement. King had introduced himself to a larger audience and received greater media coverage than he had for the Montgomery boycott. The SCLC would have an easier time from that day forward in gaining publicity and contributions.

The backlash against school integration showed the leaders of SCLC how much work they still had to do. In September of 1957, Arkansas governor Orville Faubus flaunted his intention to defy the law, standing in the doorway of Little Rock Central High School to block nine black students from entering. The SCLC began planning a March for Integrated Schools in Washington.

An attack on King nearly derailed the event. While he was signing copies of his book *Stride Toward Freedom* in New York, a deranged woman stabbed him. King's absence hurt the October 25 event, which drew only about ten thousand people. King had come to embody the civil rights movement in the eyes of the national media. The SCLC planned a second March for Integrated Schools to feature a triumvirate of black leaders: King, Randolph, and Roy Wilkins of the NAACP. Attendance doubled for the march of April 18, 1959. But when the marchers sought an audience with the president, Eisenhower refused to meet them.

Eisenhower may not have wanted to offer further legitimacy to a group that threatened the appearance of social order. The president's snub, however, only pushed young marchers further outside the mainstream. Rustin later said that Eisenhower's aloofness led to the founding of the Student Nonviolent Coordinating Committee (SNCC, often pronounced "snick"), a group whose radicalism would make the peaceful marches seem tame by comparison.

Meanwhile, protests continued across the country. On February 1, 1960, students from North Carolina Agricultural & Technical College in Greensboro went to a lunch counter and requested service. As expected, they were denied. They then refused to leave until they were served, which brought about their arrests. Others took their

The triumvirate: Wilkins, King, and Randolph. *(Library of Congress)*

place at the counter. Thus the sit-in movement began, and similar demonstrations erupted throughout the South.

The willingness of so many demonstrators to take part in sit-ins surprised Rustin and James Farmer of the Congress of Racial Equality. CORE had organized sit-ins at Chicago restaurants in the 1940s without creating anything like the national interest focused on these. The fires of the civil rights movement had grown hot, and its leaders rushed to seize the opportunity.

As the election year of 1960 approached, King, Randolph, and Rustin began planning for a march on the Democratic and Republican political conventions. They wanted to confront the major political parties with a broad civil rights agenda, demanding that the parties repudiate segregation, reduce congressional representation for districts that refused African Americans the vote, uphold school integration, and respect the sit-in demonstrators as they would labor strikers.

The planned march on the convention attracted a powerful enemy in the form of a rival African-American leader, Congressman Adam Clayton Powell of New York. For many black Americans of the 1950s, Powell symbolized success. Flamboyant and dapper, with a pencil-thin mustache, he dressed in elegant suits and drove expensive cars. For people denied economic opportunity, his success alone added to his charisma. But Powell was also vain and turf-conscious. Powell wanted to scuttle the marches and prevent any embarrassment that might derail his appointment to the chairmanship of the House Committee on Education and Labor. He sent a threat by messenger to King. Unless King cancelled the march, Powell would announce that King and Rustin were involved in a homosexual relationship.

Powell knew very well that Rustin's arrest in Pasadena would be resurrected and fan the flames of scandal. Randolph urged King to call Powell's bluff and stick to the march plans. But King worried that the young civil rights movement could be put in serious jeopardy.

Rustin realized it was up to him to quell the controversy. He resigned as King's assistant and severed his relationship with the SCLC. The planning went on without him, but the march did not succeed nearly so well as the others. Rustin and his supporters wondered if things might have turned out differently if a threat about his sexuality had not denied the SCLC his talents.

Ten

March on Washington

After Rustin quit the Southern Christian Leadership Conference, he went back to his regular duties at the War Resisters League. Sometimes he organized and other times he did the unglamorous work, stuffing envelopes and carrying bundles to the post office. But it hurt him terribly to have to stand aside just as the civil rights movement began to bear fruit.

"Bayard spent the most miserable time I have ever seen during those months," one of his coworkers at WRL recalled. "He was completely demoralized. . . . I hadn't seen Bayard except in the jail period so destroyed."

But Rustin still considered himself in the mainstream of civil rights. In a series of debates, he took on Malcolm X, leader of the Nation of Islam, a religious order also known as the Black Muslims that fought integration as fervently as white segregationists did. They also observed the more common practices of world Islam, such as refraining from eating pork or drinking alcohol.

Malcolm X, born Malcolm Little, had joined the Nation of Islam while serving time in prison. He changed his name to X to show that his real name had been lost generations ago when his ancestors had become slaves. Energetic and mesmerizing as a public speaker, Malcolm looked almost like a young college professor with his slim build and horn-rimmed glasses. But his debate style was hot, acid, laced with sarcasm against whites and the current system. Rustin had met him in the late 1950s, and the two had talked cordially. Offstage, there was little friction between them, as when Rustin asked Malcolm if he would debate him at Howard University.

"I told Malcolm," Rustin said, "that I could arrange his appearance on campus, but strictly on my terms. 'What are your terms?' he asked. I said 'We'll have a debate. You'll present your views, and then I'll attack you as someone having no political, social, or economic program for dealing with the problems of blacks.' He said 'I'll take you up on that.'"

Rustin opened the debate by saying, "The United States belongs to no particular people, and in my view the great majority of Negroes and their leaders take integration as their key word—which means that rightly or wrongly they seek to become an integral part of the United States. We have, I believe, much work yet to do . . . but I believe we have reached the point where most

Negroes, from a sense of dignity and pride, have organized themselves to demand to become an integral part
of all the institutions of the U.S."

As one audience member remembered, "Malcolm
then took the floor, launched into his Black Nationalist
message, and, astonishingly, turned the audience around.
In an electrifying performance, he articulated many of
the things that weren't being openly said by the black
middle class; and he did so in such a biting and uncompromising style that he had the audience literally shouting."

Black nationalism, in its simplest terms, proposed
that African Americans create a separate nation in order
to avoid the loss of their identity in a predominantly
white America. One of their famed slogans was "Black
is beautiful." Malcolm hammered out a far more extreme

Malcom X and Rustin preparing for their debate at Howard University in 1961.
(Courtesy of the Moorland-Springarn Research Center, Howard University Archives.)

position, denouncing not only integration but also racial equality, declaring that whites were inherently evil. He defended the use of violence, later rationalizing the assassination of President Kennedy as a natural consequence of the bloodshed characteristic of white rule. Even in the volatile 1960s, many African-American leaders considered his views extreme.

While Rustin rejected Malcolm's black nationalism, he worked for self-rule in African nations. During his three-year exile from the civil rights movement, he served as a counselor to independence movements in Tanzania and Northern Rhodesia (now Zambia), spending most of 1961 and 1962 there. The Northern Rhodesian independence leader was Kenneth Kaunda, who formed the World Peace Brigade against the ruling British. Rustin did work there he could not do in the United States, organizing marches and rallies for the Brigade.

Rustin found working with pacifist leaders once again to be exhilarating. It always struck a chord with him when someone delivered the nonviolent message as ringingly as Kaunda did at a rally, when he declared that when the Brigade faced soldiers, its activists "will not come equipped with guns. . . . If arrested, they will sit down." The marches Bayard helped organize did not immediately break the grip of British rule. But in 1964, the nation did gain its independence, and Kaunda became its first president.

From Africa, Rustin could only watch as a generation of young black people and their white supporters openly dared the injustice of the American system. The sit-in movement that began in Greensboro had sparked waves of similar protests throughout the South. Emboldened by their success, CORE launched a series of Freedom Rides into the South, seeking to test a Supreme Court decision that expanded integration into the restrooms and restaurants serving interstate buses. Southern organizers still risked horrific violence, including rock-throwing mobs, shootings, bombings, and police-sanctioned beatings.

In the North, racial activists turned their attention to a form of segregation that had escaped media notice in the bloodier upheavals of the South. It was de facto segregation, or segregation in fact rather than law. Northern cities were segregated by such factors as housing patterns—if a neighborhood was predominately white, its school would be predominately white, and vice versa. Many African Americans were crowded into urban neighborhoods, so activists focused on changing that pattern.

To ask Rustin to witness all this from the sidelines was too much, and other black leaders knew it. It was his old mentor A. Philip Randolph who helped him find his way back into the struggle.

Rustin and Randolph met in Randolph's office in Harlem on a winter day in 1962. They discussed some of the major problems still holding back African Americans, including unemployment. Randolph was eager to see Rustin resume his place in the movement. He had never held Rustin's homosexuality against him and considered the Powell smear reprehensible.

A Freedom Ride bus that has been firebombed.

The 100th anniversary of Abraham Lincoln's Emancipation Proclamation, the document that freed American slaves, was coming up in 1963. Randolph suggested marking the occasion with an Emancipation March on Washington, an event that would unite the various arms of the civil rights movement.

Rustin was intrigued. This was the kind of event for which he had prepared his entire career. The marches of 1941 and 1948 had been called off. The marches of the 1950s had been merely dress rehearsals. A united march of civil rights groups under a single banner could show the world how powerful the struggle had become.

With Randolph's blessing, Rustin set about organizing the event. James Farmer of CORE and John Lewis of SNCC embraced the idea as enthusiastically as Rustin had. Martin Luther King was initially reluctant. But Rustin continued to push, and the SCLC leaders eventually agreed to the Randolph-Rustin march. King's only request was to change the name to the March on Washington for Jobs and Freedom. That was a small concession for the two original planners, since economic equality had been the point that sparked their first discussion.

Rustin and King had wanted the march to incorporate acts of civil disobedience in the tradition of Gandhi. But both Roy Wilkins of the NAACP and Whitney Young of the National Urban League (a social service agency) wanted none of the marchers to break the law. Rustin and King conceded, and so the requirement that the march be law-abiding went into the blueprint.

Both Wilkins and Young agreed Randolph should act as official director. Randolph acquiesced on the condition that Rustin would be his working deputy. They accepted that arrangement, and Rustin found himself officially resurrected from obscurity.

He also found himself facing a task almost as complex as staging a presidential inauguration. With the date set for August 28, 1963, he knew the marchers would probably have to deal with intense summer heat. On top of that were the usual concerns accompanying any large influx of people into a city: how would they be transported, fed, housed, attended to if they fell ill, and directed from one point to another? These were the kind of questions that others considered nightmarish,

Rustin in his office during the organization of the march. *(Courtesy of Getty Images.)*

but Rustin found the challenge perfectly suited to his talents as a nuts-and-bolts organizer.

Rustin's office in Harlem resembled a war room. He was constantly on the phone, chain-smoking as he talked to reporters and heads of the various civil rights groups. Staff bustled around him, putting in sixteen-hour days printing manuals, writing releases, stuffing envelopes, and mapping travel routes. Money had to be found to pay for publicity, travel, printing costs, sanitation, and so on—a list that seemed almost as long as the march itself. A visiting government official compared Rustin's office to the strategy center for the largest European battle of World War II, writing that it was "just like they were getting ready for D-Day in Normandy." Indeed, the crowd targeted by the march group rivaled that of an army, with the organizers hoping to produce 250,000 people. They told the press that they expected only 100,000, in order to keep expectations down.

In the spring of 1963, a bloody spectacle in Birmingham, Alabama, played across American television screens as police tried to thwart a desegregation campaign led by King. The public saw the officers of police chief Bull Connor train fire hoses on the demonstrators, turn attack dogs loose on them, and shock them with electric cattle prods. President John F. Kennedy watched the carnage as well and wondered if a Washington march would create scenes as memorably ugly in the capital. He called civil rights leaders for a Saturday morning meeting at the White House.

Kennedy told them a march would threaten a civil rights bill he had before Congress: "He believed not only was there an inherent danger in [the march], but that it just couldn't possibly succeed," recalled John Lewis of SNCC. Kennedy "started saying that this march would hurt his proposed legislation. . . . He was so afraid

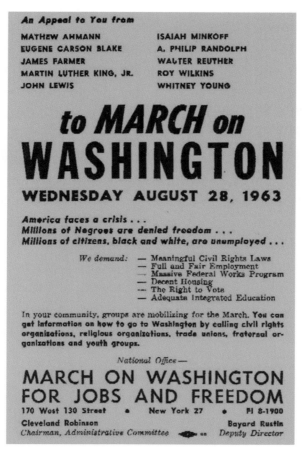

An Appeal to You from

MATHEW AHMANN
EUGENE CARSON BLAKE
JAMES FARMER
MARTIN LUTHER KING, JR.
JOHN LEWIS

ISAIAH MINKOFF
A. PHILIP RANDOLPH
WALTER REUTHER
ROY WILKINS
WHITNEY YOUNG

to *MARCH* on
WASHINGTON

WEDNESDAY AUGUST 28, 1963

America faces a crisis . . .
Millions of Negroes are denied freedom . . .
Millions of citizens, black and white, are unemployed . . .

We demand: — Meaningful Civil Rights Laws
— Full and Fair Employment
— Massive Federal Works Program
— Decent Housing
— The Right to Vote
— Adequate Integrated Education

In your community, groups are mobilizing for the March. You can get information on how to go to Washington by calling civil rights organizations, religious organizations, trade unions, fraternal organizations and youth groups.

National Office —

MARCH ON WASHINGTON
FOR JOBS AND FREEDOM

170 West 130 Street   ●   New York 27   ●   PI 8-1900

Cleveland Robinson
Chairman, Administrative Committee

Bayard Rustin
Deputy Director

A promotional poster for the March on Washington. Rustin's name is found at the bottom right in significantly smaller print than his colleagues. *(JFK Library, Boston)*

there was going to be disorder and all types of trouble was going to take place in the capital and there would be no type of legislation passed."

The others looked to Randolph to respond. He calmly told President Kennedy that the march would proceed as planned, and the other leaders closed ranks behind him.

Rustin tuned out such distractions as he concentrated

on identifying every possible problem before it happened. His beehive office swarmed with staffers eating
meals at their desks while telephones rang, as he mapped
out every challenge of bringing hundreds of thousand
of people into Washington in the heat of August.

"We planned out precisely the number of toilets that
would be needed for a quarter of a million people," he
recalled, "how many blankets we would need for people
who were coming in early . . . how many doctors, how
many first aid stations, what people should bring with
them to eat in their lunches. Plan it so that everybody
would come into Washington after dark the night before,
and everybody be out of Washington on sundown the
day of the march. We had, of course, to have fantastic
planning of all the parking lots for the thousands of
buses and automobiles."

In the back of his mind, of course, Rustin knew that his
work on the march made him a perfect target for those who
wished to derail it by any means. Senator Strom Thurmond
of South Carolina, one of the nation's most fervent segregationists, was just such an enemy, and he sprang an
ambush on the Senate floor just two weeks before the event.

Senator Thurmond made public Rustin's long arrest
record, with emphasis, of course, on the conviction in
Pasadena. He called Rustin a sexual pervert and bran-
dished a copy of his arrest record. It would have taken
a skilled investigator to get access to such records, and
many in the movement suspected Thurmond had col-
laborated with the FBI. It was widely known that FBI

Director J. Edgar Hoover had little love for civil rights leaders, particularly King, and considered the movement subversive. Even so, Thurmond's charges got big play in the national press.

A. Philip Randolph held a press conference in New York. While others had deserted Rustin in the face of the then-devastating charges of homosexuality, Randolph stood firm. "I speak for the combined Negro leadership," he said, "in voicing my complete confidence in Bayard Rustin's character. . . . I am dismayed that there are in this country men who, wrapping themselves in the mantle of Christian morality, would mutilate the most elementary conceptions of human decency, privacy, and humility in order to attack other men."

It was a watershed moment for civil liberty in more ways than one. At a time when few gay people wanted any public knowledge of their homosexuality, Rustin became one of the most public homosexuals in America. But Randolph's no-nonsense defense seemed to have closed the issue in the American press. Randolph's courage increased Rustin's determination to see that the march was a success.

When Rustin arrived at the Washington Monument at six-thirty on the morning of August 28, he was met with a disheartening sight. A crowd of a couple of hundred milled around the base of the monument, a far cry from the thousands he had told reporters would assemble by sunrise.

But the people were coming: police helicopters hovering over the city could see streams of cars and buses pouring into the capital. By ten-thirty, eighty thousand demonstrators had made good on their promises to march. The crowd spilled onto Constitution Avenue and pushed west, swelling by the hour. Coretta Scott King said her spirit soared when she saw a "whole vast concourse alive with 250,000 people." Almost a quarter of the crowd was white.

The march to the Lincoln Memorial was scheduled to proceed in an orderly pattern, with labor union leaders, congressmen, and marchers to arrive in prearranged succession. But the group at the Washington Monument began to grow restless, realizing that delay would push them farther back from the stage. At about 12:45 that afternoon, they began to march with no instructions, throwing the careful blueprint of the march out of sync. Rustin let the people go, realizing that there was a limit to how much a crowd's enthusiasm could be controlled. Some high-profile leaders of the movement, coming from a meeting at the White House, were surprised to find themselves following the march rather than leading it.

John Lewis of SNCC had planned a speech that would touch a very raw nerve, one that compared the civil rights marches in the South to the tactics of General William Tecumseh Sherman, who had burned Southern crops during the Civil War. "We will march through the South, through the Heart of Dixie, the way Sherman did," Lewis's speech declared. "We shall pursue our own 'scorched earth' policy and burn Jim Crow to the ground

—nonviolently. We shall fragment the South into a thousand pieces and put them back together in the image of democracy."

Patrick O'Boyle, the Roman Catholic archbishop slated to deliver the opening prayer, took offense at Lewis's fiery words. Tempers flared as O'Boyle threatened to walk off the podium. Bayard ordered the loudspeakers playing the National Anthem turned up to obscure a developing shouting match, as he tried to work out a compromise. Finally, Lewis agreed to use milder language and the bishop dropped his threat to walk out.

Lewis delivered an address that was radical and hard-hitting, but substituted more conciliatory lines for those that had offended O'Boyle. "We will march through the South, through the streets of Danville, through the streets of Cambridge, through the streets of Birmingham . . . But we will march with the spirit of love and with the spirit of dignity that we have shown here today."

Rustin had scheduled Dr. Martin Luther King Jr. to speak last, and some of the SCLC members had criticized him for it. They worried the crowd would be weary of speeches by the time the marquee speaker reached the podium. If they were, King revived them on that unseasonably mild August afternoon, delivering the "I have a dream" speech that would mark one of the high points in the history of American oratory.

King had intended to tone down his preacher's speaking style to suit the solemn occasion. But he noticed a rise in the crowd's enthusiasm when he delivered a line with the cadence of the Old Testament: "We will not be satisfied until justice rolls down like the waters and righteousness like a mighty stream."

As the crowd cheered, King relied on his instincts and left his prepared text behind. He spoke of the "sweltering summer of the Negro's legitimate discontent" but urged those serving the cause of justice "not to wallow in the valley of despair." He swept the crowd up in a soaring prophecy of a "dream deeply rooted in the American dream . . . a dream that one day this nation will rise up and live out the true meaning of its creed." He closed by imagining the day when African Americans would at last shout, "Free at last! Free at last! Thank God Almighty, we are free at last."

People in the crowd wept as King delivered the most famous speech of his lifetime. When the event ended, Rustin found Randolph at the end of the platform, put his arm around him and saw tears streaming down his face.

Randolph and the other leaders of the march met with President Kennedy, who, despite his earlier misgivings, praised their success. Rustin would receive no congratulations at the White House. Instead he did his usual work behind the scenes, overseeing the work of removing trash, scraps of food, and portable toilets from the marchers' route. It was his moment of triumph after years of banishment and disgrace, and staying behind to clean up litter did not diminish it.

Eleven

In the Spotlight

Bayard Rustin's picture, along with A. Philip Randolph's, appeared on the cover of *Life* magazine after the March on Washington. Having one's face on a *Life* cover was a glamorous achievement in that era. After working behind the scenes for so long, Rustin was not prepared for fame: "I don't know what to make of it, and I'm not sure that the sensation is entirely pleasurable."

The march had marked his place in history. It did not, however, bring a lasting reconciliation between the races. On September 15, 1963, a bomb went off in a church in Birmingham, killing four young black girls. Horrible as it was, the bombing was only one of many such episodes in a violent decade.

On November 22, 1963, President Kennedy made a trip to Dallas, trying to unite his Democratic Party in

Randolph and Rustin on the cover of *Life*, September 6, 1963.

preparation for the election. As the presidential motorcade wound through downtown, gunman Lee Harvey Oswald shot Kennedy dead with a rifle. Immediately after Kennedy's death, Vice President Lyndon Johnson was sworn in as president.

President Johnson wanted to be remembered for his achievements in civil rights and decided that he would go even farther than Kennedy had toward ending segregation. He pressured Congress to pass the Civil Rights Act of 1964 and the Voting Rights Act of 1965. The Civil Rights Act removed voter registration barriers for minority voters, prohibited discrimination or segregation in public places, and also banned such practices by schools, unions, or employers. The Voting Rights Act enacted federal elections standards to prevent states from thwarting black voters through such devices as "literacy tests" (often deliberately difficult and arbitrarily applied) and required new voting practices to be cleared by the federal Justice Department.

The bills passed under the Johnson administration signaled the end of federal tolerance for Jim Crow oppression. Rustin saw Johnson's commitment to racial justice as genuine. He believed in the president's broad social agenda as well, his "Great Society" programs intended to wipe out poverty, establish health care for the poor and elderly, and to conserve natural resources.

When Rustin survived Senator Thurmond's slander about his homosexuality, and magazines and newspapers began praising his leadership, King considered bringing him back into the Southern Christian Leadership Conference. In the spring of 1964, Rustin joined the Research Committee, a group of advisers who kept King informed on current issues, particularly those in the North. King met with the group every few weeks in New York.

Later that year, King won the Nobel Prize. Bayard traveled with King and his entourage to Oslo, Norway. In his acceptance speech, King said "I accept the Nobel Prize for Peace at a moment when twenty-two million Negroes in the United States . . . are engaged in a creative battle to end the long night of racial injustice. I accept the award on behalf of a civil rights movement which is moving with determination and a majestic scorn for risk and danger to establish a reign of freedom and a rule of justice."

King returned as a hero. When he arrived in New York, fireboats saluted him in the East River. He met a crowd of ten thousand people in Harlem, and the city presented him with a medallion of honor.

Rustin's old debate adversary, Malcolm X, tempered his views on race after traveling to Mecca in Saudi Arabia, a ritual journey required of every Muslim at least once. There he met white, blue-eyed pilgrims who were as serious in their faith as he was. The experience called him to question his earlier denunciations of all whites as "devils." Upon returning to America, he founded the Organization of Afro-American Unity, a group to bring the races together. In February of 1965, Black Muslims assassinated Malcolm X.

Rustin saw turbulence and violence as a threat to the accomplishments of civil rights. He began seeking ways to work within the political system to create change. As the civil rights and peace movements became more radical, more ready to stage public protests, Rustin changed his position on marches and demonstrations.

In February of 1965, *Commentary* magazine carried an article by Rustin titled "From Protest to Politics." He wrote that protests in the streets had reached the end of their effectiveness. Social problems in America centered on economic conditions as well as race. He urged coalitions with liberal groups and labor unions.

According to Rustin, social progressives should work

to hold together the groups in the Democratic Party that had given President Johnson his first electoral victory in 1964. "Here is where the cutting edge of the civil rights movement can be applied," he wrote. "We must see to it that the reorganization of the 'consensus party' proceeds along lines which make it an effective vehicle for social reconstruction."

This was not what political radicals, black or white, wanted to hear at a time when the politics of the left had begun to revolve around public protests. Defending the Democratic Party sounded particularly suspicious to those who were protesting America's involvement in the Vietnam War.

David Dellinger, the pacifist Rustin had defended from an attacker during a Times Square rally, now defended the street tactics of the antiwar protests. In a May issue of *Liberation* magazine, he said a recent Washington antiwar march had been more effective than the March on Washington because it made no compromise with established political leaders. Dellinger accused the organizers of the 1963 March on Washington of being too reluctant to confront Kennedy on his administration's lackluster civil rights record, creating an alliance with power that "has troubled and confused the movement ever since."

Staughton Lynd, a war-protest leader, wrote an even more scathing rebuke of Rustin in the June issue of *Liberation.* Lynd charged that Rustin was a political traitor. On the war, Lynd wrote, Rustin was one who advocated "a coalition with the marines"; as for his argument that economic issues were as important as the racial struggle, Rustin was "a labor lieutenant of capitalism." Lynd's rebuttal showed the growing tendency of 1960s radicals to paint those who disagreed with them, even former movement leaders, as enemies.

In the spring of 1965, Rustin took a leadership role with the newly founded A. Philip Randolph Institute. Primarily funded by large labor unions, the Randolph Institute sought to provide an economic basis for African-American equality. Both Randolph and Rustin sought a stronger alliance between African Americans and the unions, a position that put them at odds with some other black leaders. The organization supported labor unions in testimony before Congress and set up conferences on economic and social issues. It also branched out to other areas, however, holding voter registration drives and providing educational materials for civil rights groups.

Soon thereafter, Rustin resigned his position on the War Resisters League. He explained that he wanted to concentrate his energies on the civil rights movement, but some pacifists believed he was distancing himself from them. His old colleague Dr. King widened the rift when he came out against the war in 1967. Speaking at Riverside Church in Manhattan, King denounced the United States as "the greatest purveyor of violence in the world today." He called for a unilateral ceasefire by the U.S. and two weeks later led a peace rally in New York.

Rustin opposed King's statement on the grounds that

it involved the civil rights movement in two controversies at one time. In New York's *Amsterdam News,* he wrote, "I would consider the involvement of civil rights organizations as such in peace activities as distinctly unprofitable and perhaps even suicidal." Rustin was accused of abandoning the peace process. His opponents raised a valid point when they noted that Rustin had acted on behalf of both pacifism and civil rights in the 1940s and 1950s. But Rustin now urged young activists involved in more than one movement to separate their work for different causes, so that their messages would not be confused.

Rustin was not afraid to make other unpopular pronouncements. In 1966, Stokely Carmichael, director of the Student Nonviolent Coordinating Committee, inaugurated the Black Power movement, first using the term at a rally in Greenwood, Mississippi. "What we are going to start saying now is 'Black Power,'" Carmichael said in the speech, later saying that he meant the phrase as an alternative to the "Freedom Now" slogan of the early civil rights movement. He led his audience through chants of "Black Power! Black Power!"

The Black Power movement valued self-defense over nonviolence, self-determination and separatism over integration. King viewed the movement with some alarm, but was careful not to criticize it too severely, for fear of creating divisions. Rustin, on the other hand, believed that the Black Power movement went against the coalition building that had defined his life's work. At Cornell

University, he denounced black separatism, as well as a group of SNCC activists who tried to shout him down. During the question period, the hecklers all shouted their objections at once, trying to rattle Rustin with a din of confused noise. But he said he would not answer anyone who did not come to the microphone. When the first speaker took the microphone, Rustin put him on the spot by asking that he give his name. As his critics had to identify themselves, they became less strident and more respectful.

He dealt in a similar manner with two young men who delivered ringing speeches about "black pride" at a meeting of the National Urban League in New York. An official at Northwestern University recalled the encounter. "When they finished, Bayard Rustin said, softly

Stokely Carmichael, photographed here at age twenty-five, was the head of the Student Nonviolent Coordinating Committee. He introduced the phrase "Black Power" to the civil rights movement. *(AP Photo)*

and respectfully, 'Young gentlemen, I agree with you about the importance of pride in being black, but being black is not a program.'" Rustin believed African Americans should work to change the system rather than simply denouncing it.

Rustin was as quick as ever to accept the hard tasks in the still dangerous fight against discrimination. On April 4, 1968, a gunman murdered King as he stood on the balcony of a Memphis motel. Rustin was on a plane to Memphis when President Johnson, invoking emergency powers, ordered the plane to turn around and return to Washington. The president wanted Rustin's counsel on how to deal with this tragedy while avoiding further bloodshed. Fellow passengers watched as Rustin, looking like an ambassador with his tall, erect stature and graying hair, descended a stairway and stepped into a waiting limousine.

Johnson's aides warned him that Rustin's appearance at the White House might revive old scandals about his homosexuality, but the president ignored them. Rustin persuaded the president that the best thing he could do was to continue King's work. King had gone to Memphis to demonstrate on behalf of striking sanitation workers. Although the march had been interrupted by violence, even before King's assassination, Johnson agreed.

Rustin flew to Memphis as more than a hundred American cities broke out in riots. He could see smoke rising from Washington after his plane lifted off, and he worried about what would happen next. "The murder of

Dr. King tells Negroes that if one of the greatest among them is not safe from the assassin's bullet, then what can the least of them hope for?" he wrote later. "In this context, those young black militants who have resorted to violence feel vindicated." In Memphis, Rustin led a quiet, orderly march that was a fitting tribute to a leader who preached peace.

King's death ended an era in which the civil rights movement bore the stamp of nonviolence. His death did not quiet activists, as some may have hoped, but pushed them further toward the extremes of militancy and Black Power.

Bayard would never come to an agreement with the radicals. He remained at peace with himself, however, and made it a point to enjoy life. His collections of antique musical instruments grew, outstripping the space in his Manhattan apartment. He sold some of them and made room for new collectibles—figurines of Madonna and child, as well as antique walking sticks.

One of Rustin's last arrests came about not as a result of any political stand, but because of one of his beloved canes. In January of 1972, he was on his way to see the movie *The French Connection* with friends when a suspicious policeman demanded to see his cane. On inspection, he found that it contained a sword. He arrested Rustin for carrying a concealed weapon, a fact reported widely in the New York newspapers. The charges were later dropped.

When Rustin was sixty-five, he met twenty-seven-year-old Walter Naegle one afternoon in Times Square. The two fell quickly in love, and it would take Rustin's

Rustin and his partner, Walter Naegle. *(Courtesy of Jerry Goldman.)*

death to separate them. Even as Rustin deliberately slowed his pace as he grew older, controversy remained a part of his public life. He set off another dispute when he formed Black Americans in Support of Israel in the early 1970s. Many black Americans had no wish to support Israel. They sided with Palestinians against Israel in the Middle East conflict and felt that Jews had exerted too much influence over the civil rights movement. Bayard pointed out that Jews had also contributed much to civil rights.

Jewish people had, for the most part, strongly supported the movement. They identified with the struggle of African Americans because of their own oppression, most recently in the racist regime of Hitler's Germany. Jewish organizers had raised money for the fight against Jim Crow. Jewish activists had ridden with Rustin on the

Journey of Reconciliation and gone to jail for doing so.

Rustin told a reporter for the *Washington Post,* "What people forget is that when I was raising money for Dr. King, a great deal of that money came from the Jewish people. . . . I can't call on other people continuously to help me and mine, unless I give indication that I am willing to help other people in trouble. . . . The biggest hurt is to be called an Uncle Tom by your own people."

Rustin encountered few such insults when he traveled abroad. In most countries he visited, he was still praised for his support of nonviolence and African-American rights. As always, his first instinct was to help foster peace. He helped found the National Committee on United States-China Relations. President Richard Nixon got the credit for bringing about friendly relations with communist China, but it was the committee that helped open the door. Its members brought Chinese table-tennis players to America well before diplomatic efforts succeeded in reconciling the two countries—the move became known as "Ping Pong diplomacy."

Rustin remained close to his old friend A. Philip Randolph. As Randolph aged, Rustin cared for him as a son would—even cutting his meat into small pieces when he ate. Randolph died on May 16, 1979. He was eulogized as one of the prophets of the civil rights movement, a leader whose work on behalf of African Americans preceded Rustin's and King's by many decades.

In the 1980s, Bayard would work for blossoming democracy movements and on behalf of political refu-

Bayard Rustin in 1982. *(Courtesy of Corbis.)*

gees. In Poland, he met Lech Walesa, the leader of the Solidarity movement against the Communist regime, and counseled him on the use of nonviolent resistance. The ever-elegantly dressed Rustin made quite a contrast with Walesa, who favored worn blue jeans. Polish people sometimes mistook Rustin for an African prince.

As a vice president of the International Rescue Committee, Rustin helped lead the March for Survival to the Cambodian border. The march was a protest against the treatment of Cambodian refugees by the violent and brutal rulers of the country, the Khmer Rouge. He traveled to refugee camps in Thailand, where "boat people" seeking to escape Vietnam came ashore.

Bayard undertook his last mission in July of 1987, when he visited Haiti to study the possibility of holding democratic elections there. Upon his return to New York, he began to feel pain in his stomach. A doctor diagnosed the symptoms as an infection, probably contracted in Haiti.

After consultation with another doctor and remedies that failed to provide relief, Rustin entered Lenox Hill Hospital on August 21. Surgeons found that he suffered not from infection, but a perforated appendix. Bayard Rustin went into cardiac arrest on August 23, 1987, and he died the next day at age seventy-five.

Some of his fellow activists could not bring themselves to believe this vibrant leader was gone. Even in his later years, Bayard had seemed an energetic and ageless man. The newspapers wrote his obituaries in a manner befitting a national leader. Some of them got facts wrong, reporting that he had met Gandhi, or that a London education had given him his accent. But they all marked his life as a milestone in the history of his time. The *New York Post* noted his death as "the passing of the last great apostle of the creed of nonviolence."

It probably would not have surprised Rustin that his obituaries got some of the facts wrong. So often he had worked as a counselor, advisor, or organizer while others got the headlines. Many more people prefer to be leaders than servants of their movements. To find someone willing to offer his gifts without seeking glory is rare indeed.

Bayard Rustin knew the value of rare things. When considering the place in history of the 1963 March on Washington, Rustin said that he doubted an event so well matched with its time would happen again. "The human spirit is like a flame," he said. "It flashes up and is gone. And you never know when that flame will come again."

Timeline

1912   Bayard Taylor Rustin is born in West Chester, Pennsylvania, on March 17.

1932   Rustin graduates with honors from West Chester High School; enrolls at Wilberforce University in Ohio.

1934   Leaves Wilberforce; enrolls at Cheyney State Teachers College near West Chester.

1936   Leaves Cheyney State.

1938   Enrolls in City College of New York; joins Young Communist League.

1941   Quits YCL; joins Fellowship of Reconciliation.

1944   Sentenced to three years in prison for violating Selective Service Act.

1947   Volunteers for Journey of Reconciliation ride; arrested in Chapel Hill, North Carolina.

1948   Travels to India.

1952   Visits and advises African leaders.

1953   Arrested in California; sentenced to sixty days in Los Angeles County Jail; resigns position with FOR; joins War Resisters League.

1961   Travels to Africa to work with independence movements in Tanzania and Northern Rhodesia.

1963   March on Washington for Jobs and Freedom held on August 28 becomes largest nonviolent protest march in nation's history.

1980   Travels to Cambodia.

1981   Travels to Poland.

1987   Visits Haiti; dies in New York on August 23.

Sources

CHAPTER ONE: Morning of Freedom

p. 11, "Gentlemen, everything is . . ." Jervis Anderson, *Bayard Rustin: Troubles I've Seen* (New York: HarperCollins Publishers, Inc., 1997), 255.

p. 12, "Equal Rights, NOW . . ." Ibid., 256.

p. 12, "We are not . . ." Ibid., 257.

p. 14, "Free at last!" John D'Emilio, *Lost Prophet: The Life and Times of Bayard Rustin* (New York, London, Toronto, Sydney, Singapore: Free Press, 2003), 356.

CHAPTER TWO: Early Lessons

p. 18, "They were a fine . . ." Anderson, *Bayard Rustin,* 23.

p. 18, "drank an inordinate . . ." D'Emilio, *Lost Prophet,* 8.

p. 18, "At first my mother . . ." Anderson, *Bayard Rustin,* 7.

p. 20, "She towered . . ." D'Emilio, *Lost Prophet,* 11.

p. 21, "Bayard started coming . . ." Anderson, *Bayard Rustin,* 25.

p. 21, "I cannot account . . ." James Haskins, *Bayard Rustin: Behind the Scenes of the Civil Rights Movement* (New York: Hyperion Books for Children, 1997), 9.

p. 22, "He had ambition . . ." Anderson, *Bayard Rustin,* 26.

p. 22, "In scrimmages . . ." Ibid., 27.

p. 23, "Quite frankly, I then regarded . . ." Anderson, *Bayard Rustin,* 29.

p. 25, "I ask of you no shining gold . . ." D'Emilio, *Lost Prophet,* 16.

CHAPTER THREE: Young Radical

p. 28, "a pair of chino pants . . ." D'Emilio, *Lost Prophet,* 21.

p. 29, "I never said . . ." Anderson, *Bayard Rustin,* 155.

p. 33, "That doesn't sound . . ." Ibid., 49.

p. 37, "I used to . . ." Ibid., 54.

p. 40, "This man of great . . ." Ibid., 58.

p. 41, "By fighting for . . ." Columbus Salley, *The Black 100* (Secaucus, New Jersey: Carol Publishing Group, 1993), 123.

p. 42, "I am sorry . . ." Haskins, *Bayard Rustin,* 21.

p. 42, "That's when I . . ." Salley, *The Black 100,* 23.

p. 43, "the Communists had . . ." Bayard Rustin, *Strategies for Freedom: The Changing Patterns of Black Protest* (New York: Columbia University Press, 1976), 10.

CHAPTER FOUR: Ambassador for Peace

p. 46, "the symbolic inauguration . . ." Anderson, *Bayard Rustin,* 61.

p. 47, "If I can't love . . ." Ibid., 65.

p. 47, "It was hard . . ." Ibid.

p. 49, "Pacifism with Gandhi . . ." Ibid., 43.

p. 49, "Next to A. Philip Randolph . . ." Rustin, *Strategies for Freedom,* 21.

p. 52, "My heart swelled . . ." James Farmer, *Lay Bare the Heart: An Autobiography of the Civil Rights Movement* (New York, Arbor House, 1985), 59.

p. 54, "A Minority in Our . . ." Anderson, *Bayard Rustin,* 82.

p. 57, "Don't touch . . ." D'Emilio, *Lost Prophet,* 46.

p. 57, "And I said, how many . . ." Ibid.

p. 58, "When the meeting . . ." Anderson, *Bayard Rustin,* 90.

p. 59, "mother, an old sort . . ." Ibid.

CHAPTER FIVE: Prisoner of Conscience

p. 61, "I cannot voluntarily . . ." Anderson, *Bayard Rustin,* 98.

p. 62, "When you're dealing . . ." Ibid., 102.

p. 64, "Being taught by . . ." D'Emilio, *Lost Prophet,* 83.

p. 65, "You can't hurt . . ." Ibid., 84.

p. 65, "send him stuff . . ." Anderson, *Bayard Rustin,* 104.

p. 66, "You have been . . ." D'Emilio, *Lost Prophet,* 102.

p. 67-68, "We used to say . . ." Anderson, *Bayard Rustin,* 109.

p. 68, "Still, what is oppressive . . ." Ibid.

CHAPTER SIX: Journey of Reconciliation

p. 74, "the farther South . . ." Bayard Rustin, "We Challenged Jim Crow," Social Democrats Web site, http://www.socialdemocrats.org/jimcrow.html.

p. 74, "Please move . . ." Ibid.

p. 76, "What's the matter . . ." Ibid.

p. 76, "Their request was . . ." Ibid.

p. 76, "Whenever they emerge . . ." Anderson, *Bayard Rustin,* 118.

p. 77, "Coming down here . . ." SD Web site, http://www.socialdemocrats.org/jimcrow.html.

p. 77, "Get those damn . . ." Ibid.

p. 78, "Without exception those . . ." Ibid.

p. 79, "We are of . . ." Ibid.

p. 80, "He said to me . . ." Anderson, *Bayard Rustin,* 122.

CHAPTER SEVEN: Chain Gang

p. 81, "While there is . . ." Bayard Rustin, *Down the Line: The Collected Writings of Bayard Rustin* (Chicago, Quadrangle Books, 1971), 51.

p. 82, "I believe that . . ." Ibid., 125.

p. 84, "My answer is . . ." Ibid.

p. 85, "morally bound to . . ." Ibid., 128.

p. 88, "three times as . . ." Ibid., 332.

p. 89, "I started from . . ." Bayard Rustin, "Twenty-two Days on a Chain Gang," Social Democrats Web site, http://www.socialdemocrats.org/chain.html.

p. 89, "Hey, you, tall . . ." Ibid.

p. 89, "You're the one . . ." Ibid.
p. 91, "I wanted to work . . ." Ibid.
p. 91, "Captain Jones, I . . . you're learnin,'" Ibid.

CHAPTER EIGHT: Exile

p. 96, "My experience here . . ." D'Emilio, *Lost Prophet,* 146.
p. 98, "To our great . . ." Ibid., 192.
p. 99, "Bayard was in . . ." Anderson, *Bayard Rustin,* 154.
p. 100, "suggested that hospitals . . ." D'Emilio, *Lost Prophet,* 205.
p. 100, "We said 'We . . ." Anderson, *Bayard Rustin,* 172.
p. 101, "They were embarrassed . . ." Ibid., 174.
p. 102, "The effect was . . ." Ibid., 176.

CHAPTER NINE: Mission to Montgomery

p. 104, "Ku Klux Klan . . ." D'Emilio, *Lost Prophet,* 224.
p. 107, "It was a . . ." Roberta Hughes White, *The Birth of the Montgomery Bus Boycott* (Southfield, Michigan: Charro Press Inc., 1991), 33.
p. 109, "Bayard told me . . ." Anderson, *Bayard Rustin,* 187.
p. 109, "If in the . . ." Ibid., 188.
p. 111, "should not be . . ." Ibid., 187-8.
p. 111, "all whites are . . ." Rustin, *Down the Line,* 59.
p. 111, "I cannot believe . . ." Ibid.
p. 112, "White community leaders . . ." D'Emilio, *Lost Prophet,* 229.
p. 112, "And we are . . ." White, *The Birth of the Montgomery Bus Boycott,* 84.
p. 114, "Not one of . . ." Anderson, *Bayard Rustin,* 196.
p. 114, "I . . . felt that . . ." Rustin, *Strategies for Freedom,* 38.
p. 115, "If you, our . . ." Ibid., 200.

CHAPTER TEN: March on Washington

p. 120, "Bayard spent the . . ." D'Emilio, *Lost Prophet,* 299.
p. 121, "I told Malcolm . . ." Anderson, *Bayard Rustin,* 237.

p. 121, "The United States . . ." "Bayard Rustin Meets Malcolm X," Social Democrats Web site, http:// www.socialdemocrats.org/rusmalx.html.

p. 122, "Malcolm then took . . ." Anderson, *Bayard Rustin*, 238.

p. 123, "will not come . . ." Ibid., 218.

p. 128, "just like they . . ." Ibid., 250.

p. 128-9, "He believed not . . ." D'Emilio, *Lost Prophet*, 338.

p. 130, "We planned out . . ." Ibid., 341.

p. 131, "I speak for . . ." Ibid., 349.

p. 132, "whole vast concourse . . ." Anderson, *Bayard Rustin*, 256.

p. 132, "We will march . . ." D'Emilio, *Lost Prophet, 353.*

p. 133, "We will march . . ." Haskins, *Bayard Rustin*, 96.

p. 134, "We will not . . ." Ibid., 97.

p. 134, "sweltering summer of . . ." D'Emilio, *Lost Prophet*, 356.

CHAPTER ELEVEN: In the Spotlight

p. 135, "I don't know . . ." Anderson, *Bayard Rustin*, 265.

p. 137, "I accept the . . ." Ibid., 276.

p. 139, "Here is where . . ." Bayard Rustin, "From Protest to Politics: The Future of the Civil Rights Movement," Social Democrats Web site, http://www.socialdemocrats.org/ protopol.html.

p. 139, "has troubled and . . ." D'Emilio, *Lost Prophet*, 410.

p. 139, "a coalition . . ." Ibid.

p. 140, "the greatest purveyor . . ." Anderson, *Bayard Rustin*, 299.

p. 141, "I would consider . . ." Ibid., 301.

p. 141, "What we are . . ." Ibid., 314.

p. 142, "When they finished . . ." Ibid., 316.

p. 143, "The murder of . . ." Rustin, *Down the Line*, 225.

p. 146, "What people forget . . ." Ibid., 327.

p. 148, "the passing of . . ." Anderson, *Bayard Rustin*, 355.

p. 148, "The human spirit . . ." Ibid., 264.

Bibliography

Anderson, Jervis. *Bayard Rustin: Troubles I've Seen.* New York: HarperCollins Publishers, Inc., 1997.

Branch, Taylor. *Parting the Waters: America in the King Years, 1954-1963.* New York: Simon & Schuster, 1988.

D'Emilio, John. *Lost Prophet: The Life and Times of Bayard Rustin.* New York: Free Press, 2003.

Farmer, James. *Lay Bare the Heart: An Autobiography of the Civil Rights Movement.* New York: Arbor House, 1985.

Garrow, David J. *Bearing the Cross: Martin Luther King Jr. and the Southern Christian Leadership Conference.* New York: William Morrow & Co., 1986.

Haskins, James. *Bayard Rustin: Behind the Scenes of the Civil Rights Movement.* New York: Hyperion Books for Children, 1997.

————. *The March on Washington.* New York: HarperCollins Publishers, 1993.

Rustin, Bayard. *Strategies for Freedom: The Changing Patterns of Black Protest.* New York: Columbia University Press, 1976.

————. *Down the Line: The Collected Writings of Bayard Rustin.* Chicago: Quadrangle Books, 1971.

White, Roberta Hughes. *The Birth of the Montgomery Bus Boycott.* Southfield, Michigan: Charro Press Inc., 1991.

Williams, Juan. *Eyes on the Prize: America's Civil Rights Years, 1954-1965.* New York: Viking Press, 1987.

Web sites

Brother Outsider: The Life of Bayard Rustin
www.rustin.org
A companion site to the PBS documentary on the influential 1960s civil rights leader.

The March on Washington
www.abbeville.com/civilrights/washington.asp
This site provides photographs and a narrative of the event that came to symbolize the civil rights movement.

National Civil Rights Museum
www.civilrightsmuseum.org
The official site of the museum housed in the Lorraine motel in Memphis, where Martin Luther King Jr. was shot.

Fellowship of Reconciliation
www.forusa.org
The web site of the organization with which Rustin was involved. FOR is committed to active nonviolence as a transforming way of life and as a means of achieving radical change.

The A. Philip Randolph Institute
www.apri.org
APRI fights for racial equality and economic justice, working with black trade unionists to build closer alliances between African Americans and unions.

Index